Stress Management for Carers

Dr Ann Edworthy

D0995608

Cerebra,
Second Floor,
The Lyric Building,
King Street,
Carmarthen,
Carmarthenshire.
SA31 1BD,
Wales,
UK

Published by Cerebra

Catalogue records of this book is available from the British Library and
The National Library of Wales Aberystwyth

ISBN 0 95474334 2

Produced for Cerebra by Beadle Davies & Associates, Witney, Oxon UK
Printed by Imago, Thame, UK
Typeset by Mary Tudge
Cover design by Roger Locke Witney, Oxon with thanks to
Ambassador Printers, Swansea

Contents

Contents

There is now a free telephone counselling service available to parents and carers of children with brain injury and other neurological conditions. Swansea Institute has been funded by Cerebra to provide this service.
Please telephone 0800 043 9385 to access this service.

Whilst every care has been taken to ensure that all information contained in chapter 8 of this book was correct at the time of printing, some of the information may now be out of date. If you wish to make sure that you are being referred to the most recent up to date information, please telephone Cerebra's help line on free phone 0800 32 81 159.

You should seek professional advice before embarking on any therapies or entering into any legal agreement.

Foreword

Everyday we receive calls on the Helpline at Cerebra from parents who are doing their very best to cope with the pressures of caring for a disabled child. Raising a family in the twenty-first century is stressful at the best of times. Having a disabled child who will one day grow to be an adult can be the most demanding experience a family will experience.

It is often the practical problems that exhaust parents. The simplest task becomes a major operation. Getting from one place to another, taking the child to see a host of professionals, and facing endless bureaucracies to get proper help can wear out the most loving parent. There is also the job of balancing the attention one gives to other members of the family.

I am so glad Dr Ann Edworthy, a chartered psychologist, has written this book. I first met Ann at the Swansea Institute where she is a Principal Lecturer. Ann has for years counselled parents and conducted extensive research into the causes and management of stress.

She has put together in this book the principles of how parents can deal with stress before they experience 'burn out.' As a parent of a teenage child with Down's syndrome, I found the book filled with practical tips that are not hard to understand or to carry out. I hope you will find Ann's advice as helpful as I did.

Alex Elsaesser
Cerebra
Carmarthen, Wales

CHAPTER 1

WHAT THIS BOOK
CAN DO
FOR YOU

Living in a World of Stress

Stress occurs when we feel that we cannot cope with a situation. There should be no shame attached to being stressed as we are all likely to experience extreme stress at some time in our lives.

In the United Kingdom over half a million people working an average of forty hours per week are experiencing work-related stress at a level that is making them ill. It should not be surprising, therefore, to learn that parents caring for a brain-injured child are experiencing high stress levels, as their role as a carer involves working 24/7 – not just eight hours out of every twenty-four, five days a week.

The birth of a baby has a major impact on every family and because it involves a change in the daily routine, has the potential to be stressful. Babies are totally dependent on their parents and a child with disabilities obviously will require even more attention and care. In this country it is estimated that in each health authority there are an average of 250 families with one or more children who are disabled.

The Research Project

Cerebra, a charity which aims to help parents with a brain-injured child, realised, from the information they obtained from their members on a daily basis, that many of its members were struggling to cope. The problems appeared to be wide-ranging and at times, overwhelming. Following discussions with Dr Ann Edworthy, a chartered psychologist specialising in stress management, Cerebra decided to sponsor her to carry out a major research project which would identify the main causes of stress in the parents and, where possible, recommend ways of alleviating the problems identified.

A questionnaire was distributed to the parents of brain-injured children in the UK via Cerebra, special schools and by social workers who were willing to assist with the project. Over four thousand questionnaires were despatched and nearly a thousand were completed and returned. Approximately one quarter of the respondents indicated that they would be willing to be interviewed and consequently, nearly two hundred one-to-one interviews were undertaken in the second phase of the project.

Whilst the levels of stress reported varied greatly from one parent to another, it was evident that the vast majority of these mothers and fathers who fulfil the role of full-time carer are experiencing such high levels of stress that, on occasions, it is affecting their well being. A parent's emotional and physical health is of paramount importance as s/he is responsible for caring for the disabled child and the other family members. What the disabled child needs most is a healthy, loving parent. A parent can only fulfil this need by taking care of him/herself.

If a parent has high stress levels, the child is placed at great risk of also becoming stressed and this will create a vicious circle. The child will learn from the parents that the tendency to become stressed is a normal reaction to life's challenges. Additionally, a parent who has high stress levels tends to be less emotionally available for his/her children, is less tolerant of the children's behaviour and is more likely to have medical problems. Where the last situation occurs, the level of care for the child is impeded.

The last ten years have seen a wide range of legislation and policy initiatives regarding the level of help and support that each parent is entitled to receive from different sources. The reality of the situation, however, is that the amount of support that parents actually receive will depend firstly on geographical location and secondly on the quality of information available to them.

This book, based upon the research project, has been written to try and redress these issues.

What the Book Covers

The next chapter will outline the results of the research survey and, in particular, will identify those factors which the parents reported as being the main causes of their stress and frustration. Chapter 3 will look at what stress is and the three stages of stress. This is followed in Chapter 4 by advice on how to recognise the signs and symptoms of high stress levels. Personality type plays a major part in the extent to which pressure can affect an individual and Chapter 5 gives an opportunity for you to assess which type you are. The ways in which stress can affect your health and well-being is examined in Chapter 6. Chapter 7 gives practical advice on how to deal with the specific problems which cause stress as identified in Chapter 2 as well as offering advice in general on stress management. The penultimate chapter provides some relevant information including details on how to apply for, and/or obtain, different benefits and support and Chapter 9 gives a brief summary and the author's final thoughts. Each of the chapters is free-standing and should make good sense on its own. Therefore, you do not have to read the book from beginning to end to benefit from it. Dipping in and out should be just as helpful.

CHAPTER TWO

WHAT THE RESEARCH DISCOVERED

The Questionnaire Survey

Four thousand questionnaires were distributed to parents between September 2003 and February 2004. The results show that nearly seventy-five per cent of parents describe their general stress level to be appreciably or extremely high. It is clear from the comments made by the parents that they need help or advice to overcome the practical problems they are encountering and/or training in learning how to manage their stress. In an ideal world, professionals should readily understand the parents' plight and the resources would be made available to alleviate these problems. However, this is the real world and therefore, we need to look at the main causes of the stress and then try to identify what can be done realistically to help.

Parents were asked to indicate the level of stress caused by each of the thirty-seven factors listed in the second part of the questionnaire. (A copy of the questionnaire can be found as Appendix A). The findings show that there is no significant difference in the levels of stress reported by mothers or fathers; parents with daughters or sons, and parents with more than one child in the family. The results were fairly constant for all parents and will therefore be discussed as a single group. The

TABLE 1 FACTORS CAUSING STRESS

Factor	Weighted Response
1. Concern about child's future	2840
2. Devoting time to other family members	2480
3. Practicalities of taking a holiday	2441
4. Amount of leisure time available	2319
5. Behaviour of general public	2307
6. Coming to terms with diagnosis	2289
7. Level of responsibility in caring for child	2276
8. Level of coordination between services	2273
9. Amount of general advice available	2194
10. Concern about own health	2187
11. Practicalities of everyday tasks e.g. shopping	2135
12. Child's co-ordination	2131
13. Visiting family and friends	2130
14. Practical support available e.g. respite care	2129
15. Communications with child	2114
16. Mobility level of child	2110
17. Worries about cause of child's condition	2109
18. Child's distress	2050
19. Practical problems	2039
20. Worry that child may be lonely	2024
21. Amount of financial support/benefits	1988
22. Sleepless nights (due to 24-hour care needed by child)	1982
23. Violent behaviour	1936
24. Concern child does not have a happy childhood	1933
25. Concern that the relationship with spouse/partner is suffering	1933
26. Lifting and handling child	1839
27. Coming to terms with prognosis	1833
28. Illness of another family member	1710
29. Concern for a child's safety e.g. talking to stranger	1709
30. Communications with consultant	1664
31. Amount of equipment and space needed	1605
32. Communications with school	1494
33. Criticism from family and friends	1492
34. Communications with GP	1489
35. Criticism from professionals	1443
36. Receiving unsolicited mail etc as a new parent	841
37. Lack of understanding from employer	743

responses for each factor were weighted and then ranked to determine which factors caused the most stress. These rankings are shown in Table 1.

As can be seen from Table 1, concern about the child's future is clearly the factor that causes the most worry to parents. Parents constantly expressed their real worry about what would happen to their child when they were no longer able to provide care.

> 'Life is difficult enough for our children when we are alive and able to protect her. But there is absolutely no way in which we can rest not knowing whether she will be cared for appropriately when we are no longer able to fight for her'.
>
> A mother from Weston-Super-Mare

The other factors which cause high stress have been put together and are considered in the following related groups, which are not in order of importance (please note that some factors are relevant to more than one group): a) the parents themselves; b) relationships with professionals; c) dealing with family and friends; d) child-centred issues; e) the level of support received; f) employers' attitudes and actions, and g) practical problems in caring for the disabled child.

The questionnaire results have been augmented by illustrative quotations taken from the one-to-one interviews.

a) THE PARENTS

The main carer has to deal with all of the factors listed in Table 1 on a regular basis. Little wonder, therefore, that his/her stress level is high. It is doubtful whether s/he is able to pin-point accurately the precise cause of stress as they all have a cumulative effect and the result is the phenomenon of 'the straw that broke the camel's back'.

- Parents are worried that they do not always know when their child is in pain, is ill or unhappy as in many instances the child cannot talk. Parents clearly worry that their child is not enjoying life and feel helpless, and sometimes, guilty that this may be the case. This guilt is often exacerbated by worrying about the cause of the disability. Some mothers feel personally responsible for the disability and believe that in some way they had caused it during the pregnancy. Others worry that any grandchildren they may have (perhaps from their other offspring) might also carry the gene responsible for the disability and they feel that this would mean that they had wrecked the lives of others as well.

- 'Society' often does little to help the situation as the behaviour of the general public towards parents and the disabled child often causes considerable stress. Some parents speak of situations where members of the public were rude to them and chastised them for not being able to 'control their child'. The public often fail to understand that the disabled child can sometimes only communicate by shouting and take it as a sign of indiscipline, i.e. that the child is having a 'tantrum'.

One very distressing case was told by a mother who had taken her son shopping in one of the large supermarkets. As the last of her goods had been scanned at the checkout the mother recognised the signs that her son was about to have an epileptic fit. She threw her purse full of cash on the counter and bent down to deal with her son. After a minute or so the checkout operator announced that she must shift her things as there was a queue and that she was holding everyone up. Needless to say that mother was hurt and embarrassed and has never returned to that store. She now shops in another large supermarket where, from the outset, staff welcome her and offer either to push the wheelchair or her shopping trolley and cannot do enough to help.

- When parents request help from professionals they are devastated if they receive a negative response.

In a small number of instances parents actually feel that the professionals are working against them. For example, one parent was referred to family support by a member of social services staff after the mother had expressed concerns about coping with the child's behaviour. The mother attended the first meeting expecting to receive help and advice, but was merely told to go on a parenting course!

Mothers and fathers of disabled children are fulfilling essential roles and society, local authorities and the government need to give them as much support as they possibly can to fulfil these responsibilities.

- Everyday frustrations, often followed by sleepless nights, have a debilitating effect on parents' well-being. Similarly, if the child has tantrums or exhibits violent behaviour as a result of the disability, the parents need to be given respite to prevent their health from declining. After all, if the carers are ill who will look after the child?

> 'I love my daughter dearly but I am not sure how much more I can take. I'm on the go all day and rarely get more than three hours sleep a night and she wakes up crying and needs me to stay with her. I pray to God that someone will help us before it is too late.'
>
> A mother from Ipswich

Parents are finding it very difficult to relax for more than two to three hours every week and even then they spend the time at home watching television or reading. One third belong to a support group but find it impossible to attend meetings regularly.

They suggest different ways in which they could be helped, including:

a) being able to talk to a counsellor   (79%)
b) postal lending library   (44.1%)
c) learning a relaxing technique   (39%)

As a result of the research, Cerebra and the Swansea Institute of Higher Education have set up a telephone counselling line which is proving to be successful. The freephone telephone number is 0800 0439385 and you can either use it to talk through your problems with a qualified stress management consultant or simply to 'phone a friend' if you need someone to talk to.

Parnet (Cerebra) already offer a postal lending library and are happy to try and help parents obtain the information they require.

Several of the relaxation techniques that can be used at home are described in Chapter 7 and parents can obtain more information on relaxation methods by calling the counselling line.

b) RELATIONSHIPS WITH PROFESSIONALS

The survey results show that the professionals who are employed to help the parents, in some instances, actually increase their stress levels.

• Some parents speak highly of the medics, nurses, social workers and teachers whom they have met in caring for their child, but others are not so fortunate.

Most parents, on hearing that their newborn baby has a disability, react with shock, anger, dismay or guilt. It doesn't matter how well parents learn to cope over the years, almost all find the initial period very stressful. Several mothers told the author that they felt, 'shattered' 'devastated' and that their 'world had ended'.

Unfortunately, whilst most disabilities can be 'mitigated', they cannot be cured. The parents look to the professionals for reassurance and help to enable them to cope with the disability.

Parents often expressed dissatisfaction with the way in which the doctors had initially informed them of the disability. Several stated that they had been told in a rushed manner and were not given time to absorb the information and air their fears. Others said that they were given information which, at the time, was meaningless and in words that they did not understand.

> 'It was frightening as we were both in shock as it was and he spoke to us using medical terms. He might as well have been speaking in a foreign language as we didn't understand what he was saying.'
>
> A mother and father from Carmarthen

A few parents explained how it would have really helped if the doctors had explained that the parents' feelings of guilt, embarrassment and resentment were quite normal. The parents had been left to bottle up these emotions which, they say, made it even more difficult to cope with the situation.

Parents who had been afforded more time and helped to adjust to their new role suggested that successful early contact with professionals has had a lasting effect on their ability to cope as a carer. These more fortunate parents feel that they are working in partnership with the medics and are confident that they can ask (and will receive) advice as and when they need to. The other parents feel that they were not given enough information about the disability, the diagnoses and the prognosis. Several are still upset that they were not told how their child's development would be affected as it prevented them from planning ahead.

- A number of parents had to make the difficult decision of whether to keep the child at home or arrange residential care. What is right for one family may not be right for another. The severity of the disability was pivotal to the decision, as is the amount of space in the home to accommodate equipment. The parents recognize that it is often impossible for doctors to give them an accurate picture of the disability/prognosis, but are not satisfied that they are given a realistic picture, balanced between raising false hopes and total pessimism, which would enable them to make rational decisions on such issues.

- If the child is cared for at home, which was the situation for ninety-eight per cent of the sample, the GP is generally the first point of contact for a concern about the child's health. However, over twenty per cent of the parents interviewed felt that their relationship with their GP was less than satisfactory. The GPs often made the parents feel uncomfortable, that they were being 'spoken down to' and that their opinions were 'totally ignored'. Doctors do not appear to accept the parent's observations and feel they are being over-protective. One mother explained how, when she was told her child had epilepsy she just knew that there was something else wrong, but no one it seemed would listen to her. She insisted that further tests were carried out and the results showed that her son had cerebral palsy. Her 'gut feeling' had been right all along but no one apologised for doubting her.

Another parent told of how her GP became fed up with her for frequently taking her son to the surgery as she was worried about his poor development. The GP eventually referred her to a paediatrician who blamed the boy's lack of development on the mother not offering her son sufficient stimulation. Nearly a year later the boy was diagnosed autistic.

'They seem to hate to admit that parents may know more about their children than they do.... We have the responsibility for caring for our children but the doctors aren't interested in what we have noticed or think. It is crazy when you think that we are with the child 24/7 and they only see them for twenty minutes or so every month at the most.'

A mother from Oxford

- Multi-professional and multi-agency contacts are not uncommon and, if unco-ordinated, cause high levels of stress in parents. Most parents of severely disabled children spend considerable amounts of time telephoning one service or another to obtain help. Frequently they are told that they need to contact a different service and that they have to do it themselves as messages and information cannot be passed from one service to another. As one parent said, 'Too much bureaucracy, no flexibility and no co-ordination'.

It is extremely frustrating for parents who are trying to contact one of the professional groups to be continually told that the person they need is 'out' 'in a meeting' or 'unavailable'. It is equally stressful for parents to be passed from one department to another with no one able to deal with a telephone enquiry. This results in stress levels increasing when parents perceive that they are not making progress with the issue. On other occasions, parents are told 'not enough money and resources' or 'others are in the same boat'. Neither of these comments helps to deal with the issue and shows no empathy at all with the parents. Furthermore, parents are often upset and frustrated when they have to repeat the same information to each professional they meet – sometimes to two or three in a week.

> 'Why can't we have a file to take with us as it hurts to keep going over the same old problems. It only reinforces that we really aren't getting anywhere.'
>
> A mother and father from Wiltshire

- Parents of a disabled child are likely to have to make many visits to hospitals and clinics in order for their child to have tests and treatments as well as regular consultations to monitor the child's progress. They may also have to cope with their child being hospitalised. Do they stay at the hospital and leave the rest of the family to fend for themselves or leave the child in hospital alone? It helps, the parents say, if they are told in advance exactly what to expect at each appointment so that they can, wherever possible, prepare the child for what will happen. Parents need to be told, in a letter if necessary, information such as which tests will be carried out; what will happen during the procedure; what will the results tell them and so on.
- The majority of parents are satisfied with the relationships they have with the headteachers and teachers responsible for their children's education. The teachers are definitely, it is felt, interested in the child's welfare and take a personal interest in his/her progress. The only real cause for complaint is the distance some of the children have to travel to receive appropriate schooling.
- Relationships with social workers are not as good. Less than half of those interviewed had seen a social worker in the previous twelve months and some had never met a social worker. Sixty per cent did not even have a key worker.

'It took four years before I even met a social worker and since then there has been some talk and no action.'

A mother from Bristol

Social workers are **the** group of professionals that cause the most stress in parents as they either are not in regular contact with the families or do not seem actually to do anything to improve the situation.

- In summary, parents need to have good working relationships with the professionals that are charged with helping them to care for their children. Good communication skills are paramount, as is the need for adequate information and the need of the professionals to be sensitive to the parent's needs.

c) ISSUES RELATING TO FAMILY AND FRIENDS

- Being a carer 24/7 often results in feelings of guilt due to the lack of time available for the parent to devote to other family members. The lack of respite care is a real problem as it prevents the rest of the family enjoying a break where no one has the responsibility of full-time caring for the disabled child and everyone can relax and 're-charge their batteries'.

  Over fifty per cent of carers who had partners/spouses were worried that they did not spend enough time with them and were aware of the strain that the situation was putting on their relationship. Many marriages/relationships had indeed broken up because of the pressure. Also, there is a feeling of guilt that if anyone else in the family becomes ill, they are not given the amount of care they should receive as there is not enough time.

- Families feel isolated as caring for a disabled child limits the amount of leisure time for socialising. Also parents often miss the chats with other parents at the school every morning when delivering the child and in the afternoon when collecting the child, as the disabled child may have to attend a school miles away from home. This means that social contact with other similar families may be restricted.

- Most childcare provision is found to be inadequate at all times and almost non-existent during the school holidays in some areas. This again has a detrimental effect on the amount of leisure time available to parents. Family, friends and neighbours often try to help by offering to baby-sit or child-mind, but in many cases this isn't feasible as the carer needs to have received specialist training in lifting and handling the child or giving medication.

- Even when the parents are able to take time out for themselves they can rarely relax.

> 'If I do manage to get an hour or two for myself I usually spend it worrying whether he is ok. I often 'phone home two or three times in an hour just to check on things.'
>
> A mother from Neath

The alternative is for parents to take the child with them and perhaps only to visit friends or family. Those they are in regular contact with and are familiar with the child's problems are more accepting of the situation. Others who are more distant often show discomfort in trying to deal with the situation which, the parents say, often results in them trying to limit their contact in order to avoid potentially embarrassing situations.

- Another distressing factor is that on occasions any other able children in the family are cruelly teased about their brother/sister's disability and two mothers had had to deal with bullying at school.
- Most of us turn to our family and friends when we are faced with problems or need cheering up. It appears that parents of a brain-injured child can be denied this form of comfort as the very people they are turning to for support sometimes give criticism which only adds to the stress.

> 'It hurts when relatives and friends tell me I am not doing things right. It is easy for them to suggest ways of disciplining him or even what food I should give him – they don't have to cope with the tantrums and distress several times a day.'
>
> A mother from Watford

It is evident that the parents need a support group, whether it be family, friends or others in a similar situation. If the last is the preferred solution, the establishment of such a group needs to be externally facilitated because the one thing the vast majority of parents lack is time.

d) CHILD CENTRED ISSUES

This section looks at the factors most directly linked with the child's disability and which often cause parents worry and stress. It must be remembered, however, that the parents are invariably more than happy to cope with the situation as the pleasure gained from having the child far outweighs the stress involved.

- The mobility level of the child, his/her co-ordination and the ease of communication with the child only causes stress when parents are afraid that the child is so restricted that it is making them unhappy. This is particularly so when the child cannot talk because parents are never certain if their son/daughter was happy, in pain, lonely or whatever. As one mother and father from Bristol said:

> 'We just hope we have got it right. We feed her when we think she is hungry. It is too awful to even consider that she might need a cuddle and we simply don't understand and she is left feeling we don't love her.'
>
> A mother from Bristol

- Concern is also expressed with regard to lifting and handling the child.

> 'When she is in hospital or at school, there are always two people to lift and handle her. At home there is only me and I really struggle. It seems the Health and Safety Regulations only apply outside the home.'
>
> A mother from Durham

Where the disability means the child is in pain even the more basic tasks, such as dressing, can be heart-breaking for the parents. Many said that the situation improves as they become more confident but there is always a nagging doubt as to whether they are actually inflicting additional pain onto their offspring.

- Similarly, administering the necessary medicines and therapies – sometimes three or four times a day – can be wearing. Few children like swallowing medicine and cannot understand that their parents have their well-being at heart. It is easy to understand why those parents who have to administer injections and/or other procedures can become very distressed as they fear their child does not understand that the last thing his/her parent wishes to do is to inflict more pain and suffering.

> 'It tears me apart every time I have to push a needle into his skin. I pray to God that he knows I am doing it because I love him.'
>
> A mother from North Wales

- In cases where the child has a brain injury but no physical disabilities, the parents are frequently worried about the child's safety. When the child, especially a girl, becomes physically mature, parents are worried that others will take advantage of her. Parents also worry that younger disabled children, who are very outgoing and friendly, may be more susceptible to the attention of paedophiles. The children often do not understand the concept of danger and this places even more responsibility on parents who do not wish to be overly protective but know that they must constantly monitor their child's safety. This can limit the amount of freedom that can be given to the child. It is very stressful for parents to witness their child's unhappiness at seeing or hearing about their friends going out to play or to the cinema and not being allowed to participate.
- In some cases the child is prevented from mixing with others of his/her own age. There are currently very few areas where provision is made for disabled children to join play

schemes and similar activities during the school holidays (which helps to explain why the school holidays are found to be the most stressful time by nearly one third of the parents). This serves to exacerbate the feeling of isolation and loneliness and, in turn, increases parental stress. Also, the fact that the child may have to be 'bussed' to a school several miles away makes it difficult for him/her to be with friends in the evenings or at weekends unlike their siblings who would usually live within walking distance of their schoolmates.

e) LEVEL OF SUPPORT

The Joseph Rowntree Foundation Findings Report* suggests that it costs three times more to look after a disabled child than it does to care for an able child. Typically, families with a disabled child are at a financial disadvantage which adds to their stress. The parents in the survey reported that the amount of financial support was a cause of stress for them and mentioned additional laundry, heating and transport costs as impacting heavily on their family incomes.

• A number of families said that they had been forced into debt as the benefits they received did not meet the needs of the child's disability. It also appears that the government thinks that costs diminish if the child goes into hospital for a period of time because financial benefits are stopped. This is not the case.

> 'Our financial help was stopped when our son was in hospital, yet it actually cost us more. We travelled to see him every day, made extra telephone calls and had additional laundry.'
>
> A mother from north London

* Paying to Care: The Cost of Childhood Disability ISBN 1-899987-75-4

It is clear that many parents had received no help in determining the benefits and help they were entitled to and which would help them to care for their disabled child and make their own lives a little easier.

'I am seventy years old this year and I look after my thirty-nine year old son who has Down's Syndrome.
It exhausts me as it is a full-time job.
However, I can't get a carer's allowance because I receive a pension.
It doesn't make sense does it?"

A mother from mid Wales

- Parents said that it was a lottery whether you ever got to find out what benefits were available. Most learned from other parents.

'The professionals don't tell us what we can apply for ... you would think it was their own money being spent and they don't want anyone to know about it.'

A mother from Exeter

- Similarly it was just as difficult for parents to obtain information about locally based services and benefits. One parent summarized the views of many as, 'We feel we are living in a vacuum'. Another said, 'It could have been so different if only someone had told me that I was entitled to benefits ... I should have had a social worker to help me from the beginning ... I shouldn't have been paying for nappies for the last seven years when I could hardly afford enough food for myself.' It was not just financial losses which were caused by the lack of information. One mother wrote, 'I might still be married if we had been told about the help we were entitled to at the beginning. It took me having a breakdown and being hospitalized before we got any help.'

• A further problem was having to complete full and detailed assessment forms every time parents needed to apply for a different benefit. This repetition is stressful because it involves going through harrowing details time after time.

'Without a miracle the diagnosis and prognosis aren't going to change. My daughter couldn't walk last year, can't walk this year and is never going to walk. Why do I have to keep writing this and upsetting myself over and over again?'

A mother from Birmingham

• Having completed and returned the appropriate form(s) the parents often receive a visit from a representative from the local Social Services Department.

Several parents made the point that hopes are raised when staff from Social Services visit and then suggest ways of overcoming a problem such as using special equipment which Social Services will arrange to have delivered for them. However, when weeks, or sometimes months, go by without news of any progress, parents become disappointed and frustrated. In one case a social worker did not make contact with the family until the child was two years old. She then arranged for someone to call to organize having a purpose-built cot/bed for the child. The parent's initial excitement and optimism waned as nothing seemed to be happening and there was no date given for the delivery of the item. When the cot/bed eventually did arrive it had taken so long that the child had grown too large for it!

• Other parents expressed discontent at the way in which a professional may visit for one hour at the most and in that time undertake a needs-assessment of the child. Often the child's behaviour during the visit is not typical but the needs of the child are still based on that 'window'.

'They should listen to us – we are with the child 24/7. How can they possibly believe that one visit entitles them to make a decision that will affect us (the family) for a long time.'

A father from Carlisle

Many parents stated that support usually came from within the family and any additional help had to be 'fought for' and it was not always provided in the most appropriate form. Each family has different needs and parents want to be listened to in order to establish the support that would be most effective. Considerable stress was often caused by the inflexibility of the type of support offered and when it was offered.

• Respite care is a means of enabling the main carer and his/her family to have a break whilst their child is looked after by professionals. The length of respite care can be any period from one day to several weeks. In truth, however, the availability of respite care (or lack of it) is a factor which the majority of parents found very stressful. A small number of parents had never even heard of it and had consequently not had a break from 24/7 caring since the birth of the child. Others were frustrated by the unfairness of the system.

> 'There seems to be no rhyme nor reason as
> to who gets respite ... your face needs to fit.'
>
> A mother from Cardiff

- Financial help to adapt the family home to the needs of the child is also not as forthcoming as parents would wish.

Many of the children were dependent on at least one item of medical equipment and their homes did not have the space to cater for it. Other families have to overcome difficulties such as small doorways which are not suitable for wheelchair access, cold and damp houses and difficult stairways. Many, however, cannot afford to pay for the building alterations themselves and have to apply for financial help. Quite often these are means-tested and subject to delays which result in further frustration and more worry about their child's happiness and comfort. Delays in the decisions on their applications for assistance also means that the parents are living in a state of uncertainty and are not able to make informed decisions as to whether they should start applying for financial loans and risk coping with (more) debt.

Parents clearly are receiving different amounts of information dependent upon where they live and whom they come into contact with. They all need to know what benefits are available and how to apply for that help. It is clearly unfair that they have to rely on luck as to what information and help they receive.

f) THE EMPLOYERS

The vast majority of the parents who completed the questionnaires were not in regular, full-time employment and therefore experienced few problems due to a lack of understanding from their employer. One mother, however, is extremely distressed because of her employer's lack of empathy to the situation she is now having to cope with. Her child has contracted brain injury through an illness and is requiring a lot of care. The mother was working full-time before the child's illness. As soon as the medics gave the diagnosis and prognosis she asked her employer if she could be allowed to work temporarily on a part-time basis and be paid accordingly. The employer was not sympathetic and thereby significantly increased the mother's distress.

Whilst the mother may ultimately win an Employment Law case she is, in the meantime, suffering unwarranted high levels of extra stress.

Another mother had similar problems and because her health was suffering she handed in her resignation. When she felt better she sought new part-time work but faced rejection when she stated her situation and asked for flexibility in her working conditions.

> 'I was prepared to accept a job for which
> I was grossly over-qualified just so
> that I could earn my own money and
> mix with others for a
> few hours a day.'
>
> A mother from Brighton

She, and many like her, have decided not to work as the constant arguments with employers just added to their problems. This means that there is a pool of talented people who could contribute to society but are denied the opportunity because of their domestic situations.

24

g) PRACTICAL PROBLEMS

We would all like to believe that disability is now less of a taboo subject than it has been over the last fifty years or so. Legislation strives to create a culture that treats disabled and able individuals as equals. It seems, however, that to date, this has not extended to holiday arrangements. Parents find the practicalities of taking a holiday to be very stressful and the majority reported that they had not had a proper family holiday since the birth of their disabled child. There is, they say, little holiday accommodation equipped to take wheelchairs and medical equipment and able to cater for special dietary needs. In addition, often the amount of specialist equipment needed for the disabled child makes it impossible to travel to the holiday destination by family car. The parents did praise some of the rail and bus companies for the level of support they offered but, nevertheless, a journey by public transport is often too long to contemplate.

> 'Because we can't find anywhere equipped to take my daughter for a holiday, the entire family suffers. It breaks my heart when her sisters cry because they can't have a holiday like their friends.'
>
> A mother from Merthyr

- For many families with a disabled child, the lack of accessible transport often means exclusion from activities which are commonplace for most people, such as shopping. There can also be the additional problem of some members of the public or shop assistants who have no understanding of the situation and can be critical or even rude to the parents. Comments such as 'I am fed up with people giving me nasty

25

looks and some even making nasty comments that I can't discipline my own child,' illustrate these feelings. This often results in the parents taking the child out less often and therefore limiting that child's experience of life outside the immediate family and school.

- Children are learning the skills for life. These include practical skills which involve the development of physical strength and the learning of procedures. Social skills involve learning behaviour that is acceptable to society. Intellectual skills involve thinking and reasoning. Emotional development involves the balance and control of feelings. Moral skills involve the development of an awareness and respect for the needs of others. Children with special needs require extra support to learn these skills and, sadly, often experience pity, being patronised, or being ignored – all of which cause further stress for the parents who have to witness the way that their child is being treated.

CHAPTER 3

WHAT IS
STRESS?

When asked to define the term 'stress' most people will give answers that include negative descriptors, e.g. too much work, not enough time, not enough sleep, poor health. For many, the term is synonymous with worry – worry over money, health, work, relationships and so on. The list is almost endless but it rarely, if ever, contains anything positive. This is a total misconception. Stress can act as a motivator and regular exposure to stress, at manageable levels and in the right context, is good for you.

If we are to enjoy life we need to have challenges that we can achieve. Therefore, some stress is healthy and should be viewed in a positive manner. This 'good' stress is known as **eustress** and energises us psychologically and physically. It motivates us. Once we have met the challenge we feel good, relaxed and contented.

Humans need to go regularly beyond their capabilities as, each time you do this successfully, you improve your resilience to stress in general. It is when we are faced with extra challenges that we feel we cannot cope, we experience the bad type of stress, **distress**.

Stress in Parents

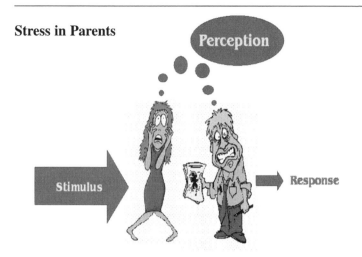

The diagram shows that increases in our stress levels are caused by the way we perceive situations and not by how threatening they are in reality.

Selye's General Adaptation Syndrome

Our Body's Triphasic Response to Pressure

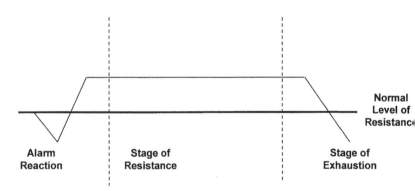

Selye suggested that there are three distinct bodily responses to stress. These are explained in the next section.

28

Stages of Stress

STAGE 1 **MOBILISING ENERGY** **'FIGHT OR FLIGHT'** **Short Term**	• Running for a bus Christmas shopping Meeting a deadline
STAGE 2 **CONSUMING ENERGY** **Long Term**	• I have to ...... Heavy workload I can't escape from .....
STAGE 3 **DRAINING ENERGY** **ILLNESS**	• I am suffering from stress – leading to illness and possibly death

The Three Stages of Stress

Stress follows the same pattern as other illnesses in that it can be acute or chronic. Acute stress is common and occurs when we are put under pressure for a short period of time. This may happen when we have extra tasks to perform or when we are not well. The term 'chronic stress' is applied when the situation becomes a continual grinding process and it wreaks havoc through long term attrition. It can occur when the individual simply cannot see his/her way out of the situation. It can also be the result of a series of minor stressors (i.e. anything which causes stress) occurring without time in between each to allow you to recover fully.

Fortunately there are three clear stages of stress and, provided we understand what is happening to us when the pressures increase, we can learn to control the overall stress and remain healthy.

Stage 1 – Alarm Stage

The first response the body makes to pressure is an alarm reaction and it will occur when the individual perceives him/herself to be in a threatening situation. The brain senses the potential danger and triggers a release of adrenaline to enable the individual to 'Fight' or 'Flight'.

When threatened, the individual quickly assesses the situation and decides whether to fight or take flight. The 'stress hormone', adrenaline, is released and physiological changes begin to take place. There is an immediate increase in energy which enables the individual to perform feats far beyond his/her normal capacity. It has been known, for instance, for one person to lift a car single-handed to free someone trapped underneath.

No doubt when first seeing the person trapped under the vehicle, the rescuer's body entered into a stress reaction. Their muscles would tense and their heart rate and breathing rate would increase. Twenty minutes or so after the rescue operation has occurred, their body would be returning to normal. The stress reaction would have served its purpose – it provided the necessary energy to deal with the situation. This reaction is

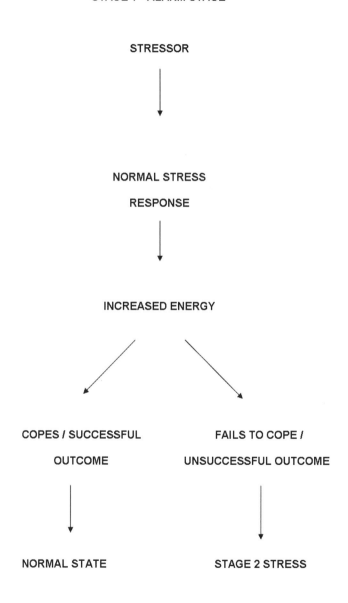

STAGE 1 - ALARM STAGE

STRESSOR

NORMAL STRESS

RESPONSE

INCREASED ENERGY

COPES / SUCCESSFUL

OUTCOME

FAILS TO COPE /

UNSUCCESSFUL OUTCOME

NORMAL STATE

STAGE 2 STRESS

automatic and immediate and is nature's way of helping us to survive.

This initial stage of stress is characterised by a feel good factor. You will have lots of energy and will undertake tasks at a quicker rate than normal. You will be excited by the challenges you face and will tend to eat faster or skip lunch in order that you do not waste time. It is a period of eustress and it will motivate you.

Stage 2 – The Resistance Stage

If Stage 1 continues for a longer period than your body can sustain, you will enter Stage 2 of the stress process. Your body will begin to realise how hard it is working and tiredness will result. This is often accompanied by feelings of frustration and fatigue. Whilst you may begin to feel exhausted and need extra sleep, ironically, you often find that at this stage you will have difficulty in getting to sleep and are likely to wake up even earlier than before. In the same way that a baby or young child seeks a comforter when anxious, you will look for common 'tricks'. The individual will seek indulgence in the food s/he enjoys; chocolate is often a favourite whilst others will indulge in alcohol or tobacco. The tiredness may lead to memory deficiency and very soon the person will begin to experience the physical manifestation of high stress. Headaches, migraines, upset stomachs are common, whilst the effects of the stress on the nervous system may result in leg twitching, particularly at night.

The individual will then probably realise that they are no longer coping with the situation and will begin to feel a sense of failure which, in turn, reduces their levels of morale and motivation.

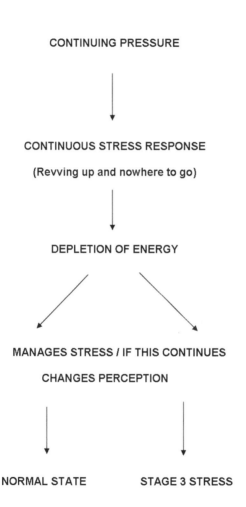

STAGE 2 STRESS

CONTINUING PRESSURE

CONTINUOUS STRESS RESPONSE

(Revving up and nowhere to go)

DEPLETION OF ENERGY

MANAGES STRESS / IF THIS CONTINUES

CHANGES PERCEPTION

NORMAL STATE   STAGE 3 STRESS

Stage 3 – The Exhaustion Stage

Everyone will spend different amounts of time at each stage but unless the stress is arrested, Stage 3 is entered. During this

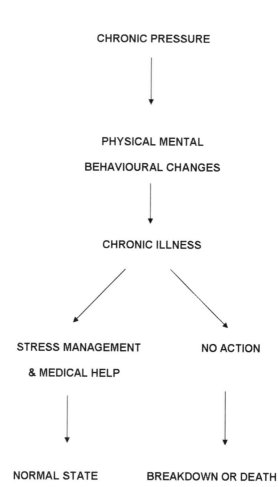

STAGE 3 STRESS

CHRONIC PRESSURE

PHYSICAL MENTAL

BEHAVIOURAL CHANGES

CHRONIC ILLNESS

STRESS MANAGEMENT

& MEDICAL HELP

NO ACTION

NORMAL STATE

BREAKDOWN OR DEATH

third and final stage the body ceases to function properly as its resources are depleted. Often the improper function of the adrenal glands leads to a drop in blood sugar levels and this leads to further disorders, some of the common ones being high blood pressure, asthma, ulcers and heart disease.

This stage of stress is chronic and causes severe health problems. It wreaks havoc through long-term attrition. This type of stress is long-lasting and has a grinding down effect on the individual as s/he is unable to see a way out of their permanently stressful life. The person is worn down to breaking point.

Stress and Performance

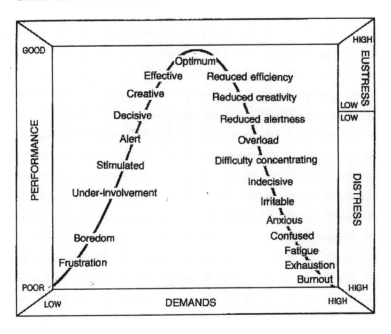

Looker, T & Gregson, O (1997) *Managing Stress Teach Yourself Books*, p75

Stress and Performance Levels

The graph shows that if too few demands/pressures are placed on us it can lead to boredom and frustration. We will be in the 'distress' area which means that we will under-perform in whatever we try to do. Once we perceive that the demands of the situation are within our capabilities and we feel we can cope, our performance improves. We are then in the 'eustress' area and enjoying the challenges we face, until we reach an optimum level of pressure. From there on, if the pressure continues to increase, we begin to feel that we are losing control and our efficiency decreases. Gradually our level of 'distress' increases, our efficiency declines and our health suffers.

It is crucial to our well-being, therefore, that we experience the correct amount of pressure. Our performance will be at its best where the demands made on us are equal to our abilities and knowledge.

CHAPTER FOUR

RECOGNISING STRESS IN OURSELVES AND OTHERS

We have already established that some stress, eustress, is good for us and without it our lives would be boring. If we do not have sufficient eustress we actively seek it. Some of us may go swimming or play squash whilst others, seeking higher levels of stress, may go parachuting or white water rafting. When undertaking such activities we would probably look and feel happy and describe ourselves as having fun. Our bodies, however, would be showing all the physiological signs of high stress levels. Clearly the difference is because in these situations we are in control – we have chosen to do them.

However, sadly, we cannot just spend our lives doing the things we enjoy. Most of us have to do routine tasks such as shopping, washing, ironing, cleaning, gardening, maintenance work and each of these activities places us under pressure. Parents who are carers have the additional problem of trying to fit these activities around caring for another on a full time basis.

The nature of the caring role means that the day cannot be fully planned as there is often interaction with nurses, doctors and other professionals, where precise timings would be impossible to pre-judge, as well as the needs of the child varying from day to day. If appointments are running late or an electricity power cut occurs which delays a meal being cooked when required, the entire day can quickly seem to become one big stress event. Unless care is taken our body's reaction to each seemingly minor problem escalates as the day progresses.

Our bodies are designed to help us cope with physical threat. We are in an age where, for most of us, our stress comes from our interactions with others as well as from the demands of modern society.

When we feel threatened our bodies respond in the only way they know – we go into a stress reaction which is a state of heightened physiological arousal. In today's society this means we spend much of our lives in an almost continual stress state. This being the case, it becomes increasingly more and more difficult to recognise the bodily stress reaction taking place and the only signs we take heed of are those indicating a deterioration in our health. Your body desperately tries to gain your attention. You may act differently or suffer physical symptoms such as headaches, nausea, dizziness etc.

Do you Know your Body Signals?

Our bodies have mechanisms to help us to stay healthy but we frequently ignore the signs. Do you:

1) Ignore feelings of tiredness and perhaps increase your caffeine intake in order to keep going?
2) Ignore the urge to 'spend a penny' because you feel you haven't got time to go to the toilet?
3) Survive on snacks because, once again, you feel you cannot afford the time to eat a proper meal?

4) Keep going even when you feel have aches and pains as you do not have time to rest?

5) Take tablets to try and keep going when you have a heavy cold or influenza?

If you answered 'yes' to any of the above you are ignoring the vital signals that your body is giving you to try and stop you before any serious damage is done. Most of us will notice any new noises in our cars, washing machines etc. and take action to try to sort the problem out at an early stage. Sadly, we are not as vigilant in detecting the signals which indicate our own bodies are suffering and many of us ignore the early warning signs until our health has suffered.

This next section will look at the signs and symptoms which indicate high stress levels and discuss the stages of the stress process when they will be most noticeable. It is very important that we become aware of our own warning signs in order to take positive action immediately. Take ten minutes to work through the next questionnaire which is designed to help you identify how stress affects you as an individual.

How Stress Affects You

Please circle the number that indicates the frequency of the factors – 0 indicates that you never experience the factor and 5 that you always experience the factor.

Recognising Stress in Ourselves and Others

		Never Happens		Sometimes		Always	
1.	I get angry very easily with the children and family members	0	1	2	3	4	5
2.	I rarely have any energy or enthusiasm to do anything	0	1	2	3	4	5
3.	I drink/smoke/comfort eat more	0	1	2	3	4	5
4.	I find it hard to concentrate	0	1	2	3	4	5
5.	I cannot relax	0	1	2	3	4	5
6.	I never feel very well	0	1	2	3	4	5
7.	I cannot get into a regular sleeping pattern	0	1	2	3	4	5
8.	I find it difficult to make decisions	0	1	2	3	4	5
9.	I tend to be moody	0	1	2	3	4	5
10.	I suffer from stomach complaints eg. indigestion, sickness, diarrhoea	0	1	2	3	4	5
11.	I try to avoid difficult situations	0	1	2	3	4	5
12.	I cannot grasp new information /ideas	0	1	2	3	4	5
13.	I often do not want to get out of bed and face another day	0	1	2	3	4	5
14.	I suffer from migraines/headaches regularly	0	1	2	3	4	5
15.	I do not want to meet friends/ family	0	1	2	3	4	5
16.	I worry a lot	0	1	2	3	4	5
17.	I look on the black side of things	0	1	2	3	4	5
18.	My heart races and my breathing is fast.	0	1	2	3	4	5
19.	I do not enjoy leisure time	0	1	2	3	4	5
20.	I do not have much self-confidence	0	1	2	3	4	5

Score Sheet

Enter your scores for each question in the boxes below and then total each section ie. add your answers to Questions 1, 5, 9, 13 and 17 together to find your total for your emotional reactions. Then do the same for your physical, behavioural and intellectual reactions.

Emotional Responses	Physical Responses	Behavioural Responses	Intellectual Responses
☐ Q1	☐ Q2	☐ Q3	☐ Q4
☐ Q5	☐ Q6	☐ Q7	☐ Q8
☐ Q9	☐ Q10	☐ Q11	☐ Q12
☐ Q13	☐ Q14	☐ Q15	☐ Q16
☐ Q17	☐ Q18	☐ Q19	☐ Q20

Total

Consider which of these total scores was the highest. This will tell how your stress manifests itself. Some of us will become more emotional whilst others may exhibit behavioural reactions. You will need to refer back to these totals when we look at the most appropriate methods for dealing with your stress later in the book.

The following are further examples of the ways in which stress can manifest itself in our emotional, physical, behavioural and intellectual reactions. The lists are not exhaustive, but will help you to see some of the ways in which your body can be asking you for help.

The Effects of Stress on your Emotional Health

Emotional Symptoms: poor concentration, inability to relax, forgetting, losing sense of humour, difficulty in making decisions, increasing irritability and mood swings.
- You may experience a general lack of self-confidence and apprehension.
- Inappropriate emotions may become evident. You may laugh when everyone else is serious.
- You could become tearful and cry for little apparent reason.
- Feelings of anger are common.
- You may panic over the least little thing.
- You lose the ability to enjoy yourself and to laugh.
- You generally feel 'low' and 'fed up' with everything.

The Effects of Stress on your Physical Health

Physical Symptoms: Headaches, sweating, palpitations, indigestion, irritable bowel syndrome, muscular aches and pains, skin irritation, constant minor illnesses.
- You may experience difficulty in breathing and chest pains may occur.
- Headaches and migraines become more frequent.
- Feelings of nausea and vomiting may occur.
- Heartburn.
- Stomach cramps and diarrhoea.
- Cramps in your legs.

- Twitching in your arms and legs, particularly at night when you are just getting to sleep.
- Feeling faint.
- Profuse sweating.
- Heart irregularities such as palpitations.
- An increase in the number of coughs and colds you catch.

The Effects of Stress on your Behaviour

Behavioural Symptoms: increasing mistakes, clumsiness and accidents, procrastinating, tiredness, nervous habits, obsessional behaviour, interrupting conversations, smoking/ drinking/eating more.

- You may dither over decisions you would normally make with ease.
- You could check and re-check whether you turned a tap off, locked the door etc. – things that you would normally be confident in doing.
- You turn to comfort tricks.
- You don't listen to other people and frequently cut across their conversation with something you have just thought about.

The Effects of Stress on your Intellectual Functions

Intellectual Function: lack of concentration, poor memory, inability to think clearly, brain will not 'switch off'.

- Your level of concentration becomes poorer and you find it increasingly difficult to concentrate on any task for long.
- Your memory becomes unreliable and you may find your-self having to write everything on paper or you will forget.
- You find it difficult, and sometimes impossible, to reach satisfactory decisions.
- Your head may feel as if it contains cotton wool – fuzzy.

- You may find it difficult to relax because you will not be able to stop reflecting on events.

You will soon learn to recognise your own signs and symptoms for each of the different stages of stress. Keep a note of the psychological symptoms such as feelings of anger, guilt, worry, shame, jealousy, fear etc. The behavioural signs may include changes in sleep patterns, comfort eating/ smoking/drinking, aggressiveness, irritability and, in some cases, you may even engage in checking rituals such as having to check and recheck you have locked the door before leaving the house. The physiological signs may be an increase in the incidence of coughs and colds, skin complaints, aches and pains etc.

You should make a note of:
- The day and time of the week;
- The situation / incident;
- How you felt;
- Your thoughts;
- How you coped.

This diary will help you to identify the situations you find most stressful. Does it, for example, come from inner personal conflicts, from sources beyond your control or because of lack of balance in your life – usually no leisure time? Many of us go into denial and try to pretend that there isn't a problem but this can lead to chronic and/or acute stress. Also, we some-times attribute the cause of our stress to respectable stressors rather than the actual ones. It is perhaps more comfortable to feel that you are stressed because of work overload rather than you feel undervalued because you didn't get a promotion you felt was due.

By keeping a diary you will be able to see if there is a pattern emerging. The exercise should not be a 'one-off' and I urge you to set aside thirty minutes to one hour every week to undertake this task. After all, if you do not identify the problem and make the necessary changes you will have to tolerate the status quo. As you become more skilled at stress management, the diary will also enable you to monitor which techniques are more effective for you in different situations (see Chapter 7). You will need to do that when you are calm rather than wait until you are very stressed and at a stage where you will not be able to think rationally. These skills will enable you to initiate appropriate techniques as and when required to successfully manage your stress and prevent it from causing you harm.

Family and friends, whom you are in regular contact with, are also able to detect changes in your behaviour often more quickly than you do so yourself. Listen to them and take the appropriate action.

CHAPTER 5

PERSONALITY AND STRESS

The ancient Greeks first used the term persona to mean 'a mask' and it later developed to refer to the different roles a person adopted in different situations. It is now used to denote the set of characteristics or traits that make each of us unique, and it is the combination of these characteristics that determines the way in which we each respond to different situations. As we have already discussed, it is our appraisal of

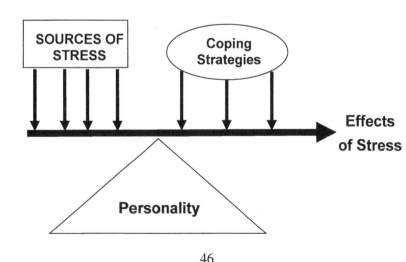

the situation which determines whether it is stressful. Our personalities, therefore, will play a significant part in determining our stress levels as they determine how optimistic/introvert/ serious, and so on, we are and, hence, the way we view different situations.

All theories of the personality strive to explain the similarities and differences in the behaviour of individuals when they interact with their environments. It is not essential for you to understand these various theories but it will help if you can determine whether you are a Type A or a Type B personality.

Are you Type A or Type B generally?

- Do you finish sentences for someone who talks slowly?
- Do you get angry if you are kept waiting at the doctors or dentists?
- Are you constantly analysing queues? – Which is the shortest / being served by the most efficient cashier and still feel annoyed if you join the 'slow' queue.
- Or perhaps :
  When you visit a supermarket to purchase three items and find yourself at the 'Express '8' items or less' checkout and the customer in front of you has nine items in her basket you become more and more anxious and even contemplate (or perhaps already have) complained to the cashier or supervisor.

If you answered 'yes' to any of these questions you tend toward Type A personality and will need to look at ways of modifying your hurried and competitive life-style.

If you answered 'no' to most of the above you are probably the person with the extra item in the checkout! You are mostly Type B personality and are enjoying a fairly relaxed life. Extreme Type A and B personalities find it almost impossible to co-operate, but must realise that none of us have the right to try and 'change' someone else.

None of us will be permanently Type A or B as we can move from one extreme towards the other depending on the circumstances. We do need to recognise the situations that make us more 'Type A' and try to overcome our aggression and anxiety and the desire to get things done as quickly as possible. In truth, it is rare that we can speed things up so it would be better to accept the delays / inconvenience and 'go with the flow'.

The Type A Personality

Type A personality usually has a chronic sense of time urgency and sets him/ herself deadlines for everything. As such, Type As have to be doing several things at once and may not have very high self-esteem. They always feel 'driven' and as a result Type A individuals are more at risk of high blood pressure and coronary heart disease. They are also more prone to stomach ulcers, allergies and poorer mental health.

Type A individuals discharge more of the 'stress hormones' than Type Bs, which makes it take three times longer for them to get rid of dietary cholesterol after meals. It is important, therefore, for Type A individuals to manage their behaviour in order to reduce the risks to their health and well-being.

Reducing Type A characteristics

There are a variety of training programmes available to help Type As to modify their behaviour. Indeed, some cardiac specialists refer their patients to such programmes as they suggest that it is their personalities and, therefore, behaviour patterns which are primarily causing ill-health.

PERSONALITY TYPE 'A'

Aggressive speech

Easily bored

Talk, walk and eat quickly

Finishes sentences – impatient

Polyphasic – does several things at once

Can't relax

Tense

Rushes

Success measured by gain

PERSONALITY TYPE 'B'

Easy going

Plays for fun

Relaxes

Efficient

None of characteristics of Type 'A'

Tactics

1. The more Type A personality you are, the less likely you are to be a good listener; you tend to speak for others, and even finish their sentences for them. Therefore, try to restrain yourself from being the centre of attention by constantly talking. Force yourself to listen to other people by remembering the axiom 'we have two ears, but only one mouth – use them in these proportions.'

2. Try to control your obsessional, time-directed life. As you are usually bad at estimating the amount of time you need to complete tasks or make journeys, you should try to identify how much time is needed, and add extra time (at least ten minutes). This will help to prevent you from having to drive in a 'white-knuckle' manner from place to place. It might also help if you carry something to read, so that if you arrive early for an appointment, you will not become impatient and feel you are wasting time. Ultimately your goal should be to try to sit, relax, absorb the environment, unwind and mentally prepare yourself for the meeting. Initially, you will find this difficult as the slower lifestyle will be alien to you, but try to build up your tolerance levels gradually by deliberately exposing yourself to situations where this is likely to happen. Use the technique of 'self-talk' to avoid becoming impatient or angry. Distract yourself by thinking about something pleasant that is going to happen soon. Make sure that you reward yourself for controlling your time-directed life.

3. Focus on one thing at a time. If you try to do numerous tasks at the same time you will revert to being time-driven.

4. Recognise that the majority of daily tasks do not require immediate action and a slower, more deliberate pace might result in better quality decisions and judgement. When you feel under pressure, ask yourself, 'Will this matter / have any importance five years from now/' Or,

'Must I do this right now?' or 'Do I have time to think about the best way to accomplish it?' Remember, only a corpse can be said to be finished.

5. Cease trying to be an idealist because it is likely to simply end up in disappointment and hostility towards others.

6. Do not bottle up emotions or anger because this is extremely damaging. Find ways to 'vent steam'. For example, engage in some vigorous physical activity that is not goal driven – I can highly recommend hitting a squash ball! Write an angry letter, but keep it somewhere safe until you calm down and can read it again. Then choose the best course of action. Talk only to trusted friends about your thoughts, fears and anxieties. Listen to their advice.

7. Learn to say 'No' in order to protect your time. Stop trying to prove yourself!

8. Take regular exercise.

9. Learn to use some form of relaxation, meditation or yoga.

10. Do not expect to change your Type A tendencies completely. This is an unrealistic and impossible goal. 'Trying to get a hare to move around just like a tortoise is evolutional suicide; just ask the fox!'

CHAPTER SIX

STRESS AND HEALTH

Introduction

Researchers have been looking at the relationship between stress and health for more than fifty years.

The stress response is programmed into our brain and we all tend to respond in a similar way. As soon as the brain senses that the individual is stressed, the hypothalamus (the master gland in the brain) sends messages to the adrenal glands to produce and release more adrenaline, noradrenalin and cortisol. This increases the activity of the sympathetic nervous system which in turn causes an increase in the heartbeat, blood pressure, respiration and perspiration rates. Concurrent to this, the blood vessels and muscles constrict giving us a tense or nervous feeling. Pupils dilate and our hearing becomes more acute to enable the individual to be more alert and to look out for potential danger.

This is nature's way of helping us to survive. Whilst this stress reaction was useful for cavemen when they hunted wild animals for food, it is not so useful in today's environment where most of our stress comes from a variety of psycho/social/emotional events. Threat has evolved and can now be constant, repeated or sudden rather than short and sharp. It is often the tensions of family life and frustrations with our careers which cause stress and in these circumstances, our stereotyped physical response, which is a maladaption, may do us harm.

The release of the hormones activates the enteric system. This is located in the stomach and works independently of the brain and nervous system. At best it will cause a 'butterflies in the stomach' sensation but can result in such disabilities as irritable bowel syndrome and colitis. Sometimes during the early stages of stress the individual may visit his/her GP explaining that s/he is not well but being unable to pinpoint the precise problem. The doctor may run some tests and pronounce the person 'fit' as the ultimate manifestations of the stress are not yet evident. If that person then continues his/her life in the same manner, and experiences the same pressure, a later visit to the GP will probably not result in similar news as the first occasion. Eventually, as the stress progresses through Stages 2 and 3, medical tests will reveal pathophysiological evidence of tissue damage and there may be a presence of stomach ulcers and blood pressure may need to be medically controlled. Unless action is taken either to remove the stressor or to control the stress, serious illnesses can result, and these can be classified into two main categories namely physiological and psychological illnesses.

PHYSIOLOGICAL ILLNESSES

Infections

Research has shown that negative emotions such as anxiety, grief and depression are immune suppressive and can lead to serious illness and possible death. When healthy, our immune system is able to protect us from infection and also prevents our own cells from developing incorrectly. The system firstly uses our skin and mucous membranes as barriers to prevent harmful micro-organisms taking hold. Should this measure fail because of surface infection or stress/traumas, the fifty billion or so white cells in our blood spring into action to destroy the antigens. In situations where the white cells are familiar with the type of antigen attacking the body, they can produce large amounts of antibody and can thereby deal successfully with the problem with expediency. Vaccinations/immunisations aid the immune system by injecting all or part of an antigen in order for the system to develop antibodies and to be able to memorise the successful antidote for future use if and when required.

Under pressure the body concentrates its energy on producing stress hormones and loses its ability to produce the chemicals essential for an efficient immune system. When the latter becomes depleted, the individual will have little or no natural resistance and will be more susceptible to coughs and colds and other infectious illnesses. It is usually immediately following a period of high stress that an individual becomes ill.

Asthma and Diabetes

Once the immune system becomes suppressed, latent viruses such as shingles or mononucleoses can become active. Non-viral diseases such as asthma and diabetes have also been linked to high stress levels. Similarly, the most common form of diabetes, diabetes mellitus, has also been shown to be significantly affected by stress as stressors can alter the body's insulin needs.

Ulcers

Peptic ulcers have been found to occur twice as often in individuals who have high levels of stress. The ulcers are triggered by the accumulation of excessive acid in the stomach, which in turn is triggered by feelings of anger and hostility.

THE PHYSICAL EFFECTS OF STRESS ON THE BODY

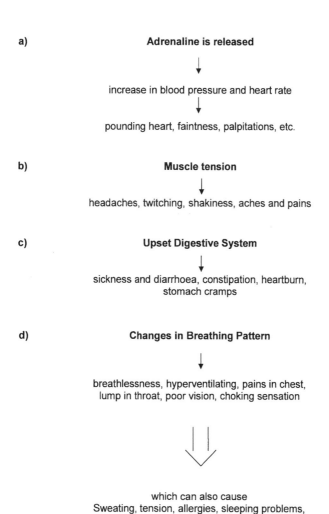

a)   **Adrenaline is released**

increase in blood pressure and heart rate

pounding heart, faintness, palpitations, etc.

b)   **Muscle tension**

headaches, twitching, shakiness, aches and pains

c)   **Upset Digestive System**

sickness and diarrhoea, constipation, heartburn,
stomach cramps

d)   **Changes in Breathing Pattern**

breathlessness, hyperventilating, pains in chest,
lump in throat, poor vision, choking sensation

which can also cause
Sweating, tension, allergies, sleeping problems,
disorientation

Stress and Health

The Effects of Good and Bad Stress on the Body

	Body Part	EUSTRESS Positive Reaction	DISTRESS Negative Reaction
1.	Heart	The lungs and muscles need more blood to provide energy when stressed. The heart, therefore, pumps faster to enable this.	Increased heart rate can result in increased blood pressure, fatty deposits in arteries, heart attack or stroke.
2.	Brain	To enable quick thinking and concentration the brain triggers the release of endorphins. (feel good factor).	Eventually the supply of endorphins is depleted which results in an increase in aches/pains, mental exhaustion.
3.	Lungs	Become more efficient to provide oxygen.	Hyperventilation which leads to Dizziness and Fainting.
4.	Blood	The blood thickens due to the increase in the production of red and white blood cells. This provides more oxygen which boosts the immune system (white cells) The spleen produces more blood-clotting agents in case of damage.	The thickening of the blood may result in clots in the arteries which in turn may lead to heart attacks or strokes.
5.	Immune System	Number of white blood cells increases which improves immunity.	The body stops the production of white cells and hormones as there is a danger they will attack their own tissue. This results in an increase in infections.
6.	Thyroid	More thyroxin is released to provide more energy.	High levels of thyroxin may cause heat intolerance; anxiety; weight loss; sleeplessness and exhaustion.

7.	Skin	Becomes very sensitive. Increased perspiration. Blood sent to major organs to limit bleeding if body is injured.	Pale and clammy. Discomfort.
8.	Muscles	Receive blood rich in oxygen and glucose to provide more energy.	Build up of lactic acid Which can result in aches and pains.
9.	Libido	Decline in sex hormones.	Impotence in men. Fall in sex drive in men and women.
10.	Eyes and Ears	Sympathetic nervous system is stimulated. The pupils dilate to provide sharper vision and the acoustic nerves are stimulated To provide sharper hearing.	Eye conditions such as glaucoma can be aggravated. Loud noises become intolerable.

Adapted from *Stressed Teachers in a Class of Their Own*
Safety Education, winter 1999 p17

Palpitations and Arrhythmias

When under pressure, our heart beats quicker and sometimes we become aware of this and state that we are suffering palpitations. If, however, the heart beat becomes irregular (we are said to be experiencing arrhythmias) which can, in some instances, prove to be fatal. Generally palpitations are harmless but do need checking out with your doctor.

Headaches

A visit to any pharmacy will confirm that a great number of individuals frequently experience headaches as there is now a vast number of appropriate over-the-counter pain killers on sale to alleviate the symptoms. The most incapacitating type of headache is migraine, which is vascular. Tension or stress headaches are the result of worry and frustration. The ache occurs when the body has an insufficient supply of oxygen to feed the muscles in the head and neck, which have contracted in response to the stress. To try to compensate, the blood vessels expand in an attempt to secure a larger oxygen supply and this causes the pain. Often the pain may be throbbing in nature and can be felt with the beat of the pulse as blood flows through the swollen vessels. Whilst analgesics will act as a 'mask' and cause the pain to subside, they do not deal with the problem. Stress management techniques will be discussed later but it is worth mentioning here that research has shown relaxation techniques and biofeedback to be the most effective long-term methods for dealing with tension headaches.

Blood Pressure (Hypertension)

As previously stated, the stress reaction causes the heart to beat faster. Normally our heart beats about 72 times per minute. Our blood pressure is given in two measurements. The systolic reading which is the pressure when the heart contracts and the diastolic reading which records the pressure when the heart is relaxed. The systolic is usually 100 plus your age whilst the diastolic is usually 80mm Hg. As we age the blood vessels become more rigid which results in an increase in blood pressure.

There is no clear cause of hypertension. It may be hereditary or it may result from being overweight, unfit, or consuming excessive alcohol. It is now evident that stress can contribute to the problem.

Heart Disease

Stress can affect the heart in a number of ways. Long term stress increases the tendency for blood to coagulate which causes a build up of blood platelets causing the blood to have to circulate through narrower arteries. In order to do this, the heart has to work harder to produce the blood flow. This condition is commonly referred to as the hardening of the arteries (or medically as myocardial ischemia). It is interesting to refer back to personality types and to note that research has now shown that those individuals who exhibit Type A behaviour patterns are twice as likely to develop coronary heart disease than Type B persons. This theory is based on the hypothesis that heart disease can be partly attributed to the cardiovascular response to stress and that Type As experience more stress generally.

PSYCHOLOGICAL ILLNESSES

The most common psychological manifestations of high levels of long-term stress are depression, burn-out and breakdown.

There is still some stigma attached to mental illness and many in need of medical help are often reluctant to present themselves for treatment.

One of the most common psychological illnesses caused by stress is depression and most of us are affected by it at some time or another, either personally or through the illness experienced by a relative or friend.

Depression can take two forms, but it is generally agreed that both occur when the individual reaches a stage whereby he/she can no longer function normally in society. It is such a pervasive illness that every aspect of the sufferer's life is affected. The individual feels helpless. The brain cannot function properly and it becomes extremely difficult for the person to concentrate on anything and to make any rational decisions. Depressive cognition is a risk factor for depression. It is characterised by excessive self-blame and pessimism. When the intensification of the feelings of 'sadness' are gradual in their onset, depression can remain undetected for some time. The problem is also masked because many of the symptoms of depression mimic the physical manifestations of stress such as sleeplessness and appetite loss. Additionally the symptoms can be so severe and disabling that the individual cannot seek help. As a result of these related problems the illness is often misdiagnosed and in serious cases thoughts of suicide may appear to be the only way out of a seemingly hopeless situation.

Mental breakdown can often be slow in its onset and is more noticeable to others than the sufferer. It may be characterised by obsessive activity such as checking all taps are turned off or persistent washing. The confused thought processes may lead the person to commit a shoplifting offence or resign from work unexpectedly. Self-mutilation, screaming, head-banging and extreme mood swings also signify this illness.

'Burnout' is a metaphor which describes a state of total exhaustion – it is the erosion of the human spirit. All of the fuel has been used up and there is no more available. It occurs when a person gives too much for too long and receives too little in return. Accountants would perhaps view it as an imbalance between investments and returns. Professional help must be sought if the condition becomes this serious and the condition is usually treated with counselling, antidepressants and/or psychotherapy.

Conclusion

Stress is mostly an experience we create for ourselves. Therefore, only we can control and manage it. Fortunately, stress management is a skill that everyone can learn.

Dozens of books have been written on stress and stress management but most contain theories and references to academic research. This book has been written to try to help parents who, because of the additional pressures they encounter in caring for a disabled child, experience high stress levels for a variety of reasons. As such, it is written as a practical guide and the theoretical aspects have been kept to a minimum.

The next chapter will, therefore, offer practical advice aimed at helping the parents to learn to control their stress levels.

CHAPTER 7

HELPING WITH THE PROBLEMS

Introduction

The research survey identified a number of inter-related areas which can cause excessive stress. In this chapter, the author deals with these problems under the same headings as those used in Chapter Two. However, in the end, they all focus on the individual parents who have to learn to manage, and preferably reduce, their own stress. Hence, the first section is much longer than the remainder as it will cover techniques that are both pro-active, to prevent a build-up of stress, and reactive, to reduce existing stress levels.

a) THE PARENTS

The most obvious way to prevent high levels of stress from occurring is to remove the stressor. This is not always possible and, even if it is an option, the stress-free condition may only be a temporary one, for as soon as you get rid of one source of anxiety, another will arrive. You will be unable to continue through life avoiding potentially stressful situations. The answer, therefore, is to look at what we each can do to minimise our stress reactions. Each person is responsible for looking after themselves. We must accept responsibility for our own health and general well-being. After all, we are the ones with the most to lose. It is our lives that are at stake.

Consider this statement:

> 'If you always do what you have always done,
> you will always get what you always got.'
>
> Walter Emerson

The message is very clear. If you are to succeed in your quest for a less stressful life, you will need to make changes.

Are you willing to make changes? Try to change one aspect of your life for one week. You may choose from any behaviour that has become habitual. You may decide to sleep on the other side of the bed, store groceries in a different cupboard, keep your car keys in a different place and so on. If you can make such a change then you are serious in your attempt to take control of your stress levels.

Change to be Proactive

There will be times when it is impossible to change the stressful situation. On such occasions we need to be as strong as possible to deal with the problems we are facing.

The next section will suggest ways in which you can become pro-active, i.e. improve your general health and well-being, which will afford you more resistance to the pressures you will face.

- The first change you must make is to improve your diet (unless you are confident that it is well-balanced and nutritional) and to eat regularly. Stress has a negative effect on our immune systems and you therefore need to do everything you can to help that system to remain efficient to protect yourself from infections and disease. When we are highly stressed and rushing to get things done, we often fail to eat properly and may even suffer from vitamin deficiency. Some of the signs of this are: a bright red tongue instead of a healthy pink one; cracked lips; dry skin; brittle nails; bruising easily but healing slowly. As well as ensuring we have meals at regular intervals we must also be careful as to what we actually consume. When in a hurry it is very easy to turn to fast foods which are often high in sugar content. Sugar provides calories but no nutrients and will raise your blood sugar levels rapidly. The body will react by releasing insulin to restore the balance and this results in a dip in energy known as hypoglycaemia (low blood sugar). The symptoms are mood swings, irritability, dizziness and fatigue. When levels are low you will behave and react unpredictably. Foods rich in tryptophan such as fish, pasta, rice, bananas, chicken and walnuts cause more serotonin to be produced and this encourages relaxation and a sense of calm.

Eating a balanced diet with complex carbohydrates such as wholemeal bread, jacket potatoes and pasta instead of refined carbohydrates such as biscuits will give your body the energy it needs to prevent everyday pressures resulting in high stress levels.

You can also help your immune system by eating plenty of fresh fruit and vegetables and it is important that you drink plenty of non-alcoholic fluids to rehydrate your body – water being the best option. It also helps to keep your caffeine intake as low as possible as it mimics the effect of adrenaline and speeds up your metabolism which is similar to the stress reaction that you are trying to prevent. And remember:

a) Sit down to eat.

b) Put everything on a plate – even snacks.

c) Don't do anything else at the same time – enjoy the meal.

d) Chew properly as this will produce enzymes which break down the food and starts the digestive process.

e) Always have breakfast as it will help your concentration and give you a good start to the day.

- Exercise goes hand in hand with a sensible diet. The fitter you are, the better able you will be to cope with potentially stressful situations and the quicker your body will return to normal after a stress reaction. Aim to find a type of exercise that suits you and make it a part of your life. You do not need to leave your own home as skipping, stretching, walking/ running up and down the stairs, are all very beneficial and can be fitted in around your other tasks. You will not have to rely on anyone else and you will not have to pay for the use of equipment.

Obviously, if you have the resources (time, money and child-minder) and are able to join a fitness club you will also benefit from the social interaction. Aerobic routines will exercise the heart and remove tensions from the cardiovascular system. Stretching alleviates muscle tension and gentle weight lifting (using bags of sugar, cans of baked beans, for example) strengthens muscles and bones, and reduces the incidence of stress-related aches and pains. A lack of exercise can make the heart flabby and the slightest exertion will then cause it to strain.

Digestive problems can be made worse and often result in indigestion or irritable bowel syndrome (IBS) and it goes without saying that a lack of exercise can result in obesity which, in turn, will lower confidence and self-esteem. Exercise will:

a) increase the body's ability to take up oxygen and expel carbon dioxide;

b) decrease lactic acid in muscles which decreases aching;

c) increase levels of endorphin and serotonin which are the feel good factors;

d) help the body to store glycogen which gives us the energy to keep going;

e) improve the condition of the heart;

f) increase high density lipoproteins (good cholesterol) and decreases low density lipoproteins;

g) keep arteries in good condition.

Please note that whilst exercise is very beneficial, it is always advisable to discuss your proposed schedule with your GP before embarking on any exercise programme.

- The third change you need to make to your lifestyle is to include more enjoyment, pleasure and laughter. Again, this need not cost money and you do not have to leave your home. Do the things you enjoy. Listen to music you like, read books which give you pleasure, select television programmes to ensure there is fun in your life. When you are happy and when you laugh there is an increase in the secretion of chemicals that improve the oxygen content of your blood. This in turn improves your cardiovascular and respiratory systems which lead to an improved immune system.

It is common for anyone suffering high stress to give up the very thing that would help them – their leisure time. All too often the individual will sacrifice the things s/he enjoys doing to devote more time to worrying about a problem. You must keep some free time to devote to hobbies and interests as they will help to alleviate the stress and enable you to think more clearly.

The old saying, 'prevention is better than cure' is very appropriate when learning to manage your stress but we must not presume that eating a healthy diet, exercising, and increasing these aspects of our lives which give us pleasure, will guarantee our stress levels remain low. There will be occasions when situations and problems will appear insurmountable and our level of distress will significantly increase.

Unless we find ways of undoing the stress reaction, our health will begin to suffer and this often results in a visit to our GP.

Doctors will treat the symptoms we describe and provide us with prescriptions for pills and potions which will make us feel better. Benzodiazepine tranquillizers and sleeping tablets are medically prescribed drugs frequently given to patients suffering from high levels of stress. Whilst in the short term they may help to alleviate the symptoms, they do not address the cause of the problem. They are temporary measures to help us to cope but clearly the real and only solution is to manage our stress so that it does not make us ill. This section looks at some of the techniques which can help limit your stress response. Once you have found a method that works for you, you will be able to manage your stress, i.e. you will be back in control.

Learning to undo the stress reaction is the most immediately effective and the only long-term solution to the problem. It necessitates learning ways to relax. It sounds very simple and therefore easy to achieve but most of us find the art of relaxing very difficult to do. How often, for instance, do you look forward to watching a television film or video but find that you cannot sit and watch it from beginning to end without thinking of the jobs you could be doing? Even worse, do you actually get up and try to do some of the jobs quickly whilst the film is playing? These relaxation activities are vital to your well-being and they must be allocated specific hours and afforded the same respect you give to other parts of your life. You will find that by doing something you enjoy, you will gain energy and thereby feel better. Sometimes it is very difficult to put down a really good book when it is time to sleep. Yet, whilst we may have only enjoyed five or six hours sleep, we wake up happy and refreshed. Enjoyment gives us energy.

Practising a stress management technique should become a part of your everyday life as it will slow down your nervous system. You will control your stress and be able to perform efficiently and effectively even when under pressure and your quality of life will improve.

Before we begin to look at the different techniques it is important to remember that we are individuals. As such, the technique(s) that will work best for us will depend on our expectations, past experience, personality, beliefs, vulnerabilities and resources.

• One of the most effective techniques is **Progressive Relaxation**. Psychologists have known for some time that anxiety and deep muscle relaxation are mutually exclusive. That is, you cannot be anxious and relaxed at the same time. This finding has been used to successfully treat many phobias, but it can also be a useful strategy for dealing with stress. If you really do want to learn how to undo the stress reaction of your body you need to master the technique of systematically relaxing all of your muscle groups. The goal is to train your muscles to be able to become relaxed on demand, thereby cutting the stress cycle short and it is one of the easiest processes to master provided you learn the technique when your stress level is relatively low. It involves taking one group of muscles at a time, tensing them for approximately ten seconds and then relaxing the muscles. This technique, once mastered, is guaranteed to relax you as it is based on the principle of muscle physiology. Once the muscles relax, other parts of the body begin to de-stress as well. The breathing rate will slow down as relaxed muscles need less oxygen. This in turn means that the heart can slow down which results in a lowering of the blood pressure. The digestive system resumes its function as blood can now be supplied to the stomach. Gradually all the stress symptoms ease and disappear. Try this yourself.

Find a quiet place where you will not be disturbed for twenty minutes or so. You should be seated on a comfortable chair which supports your back and allows your feet to be placed on the floor. Get as comfortable as possible but pay attention to how you feel as you begin. Do you have any aches and pains; do you feel anxious or tense? You must try to remember these feelings as they will be your reference point as you become more skilled in this technique.

We will begin by using the major muscles in the arms.

Bend your right hand back at the wrist and hold the tension. Count to ten and then relax.

Do the same with your left hand. Hold the tension for the count of ten and relax.

Form fists with both hands and hold the tension for the count of ten. You should be able to feel this tension spread up your arms towards your elbows. Relax.

Next, bend both arms at the elbows and raise your hands up towards your shoulders. Tighten your biceps and hold for ten seconds. Relax. Next we will concentrate on your face beginning with your forehead. Raise your eyebrows as far as you can and hold the tension for the count of ten. Relax.

Close your eyes and squeeze them shut as hard as you can and hold the tension again for ten seconds. Relax.

Next, the jaw. Bite down and clamp your teeth together. Hold the tension in the jaw for ten seconds. Relax.

We now have your arms and your face relaxing and we will now work on your neck. Bend your face forward as far as you can by trying to touch your chest with your chin. Hold the tension for ten seconds. Relax.

Raise your shoulders as high as you can and hold the tension for the count of ten. Relax and let your shoulders drop and relax.

For your chest you must take a deep breath while at the same time trying to touch your shoulder blades together by pulling your arms back. Hold the tension for ten seconds. Relax.

For your stomach you must pull it in as if you are trying to touch your spine with your stomach. Hold for ten seconds. Relax.

For your back, arch out, away from the back of the chair and you will feel tension along the spine. Hold for the count of ten. Relax.

With your feet flat on the floor, press down and feel the tension spread up the back of the legs and hold for ten seconds. Relax.

For the right thigh raise your leg up in front of you and feel the tension spread up the back of your leg. Hold for ten seconds and then relax.

Do the same thing with the left leg and relax.

Finally, your feet. Bend your toes up as if pointing towards the ceiling and feel the tension around the feet and ankles. Once again hold for ten seconds. Relax.

Now keep practising at least twice a day until you have mastered the art.

When you have used these exercises, make a note of how you feel and compare it to the way you were feeling before you began the routine. What differences do you notice? Do you feel more relaxed? If so, how do you know? Did your aches and pains disappear? If they did then they might be muscle-tension related. If your hands and feet feel warmer after the exercises it may be because of the dilation of blood vessels in the extremities, which had constricted when you were stressed. You may experience sleepiness and/or a feeling of calmness. All of these signs indicate a state of relaxation and indicate that this technique works for you. You must remember, however, that the technique requires you to learn a new skill and, as such, requires practice. It is vital that this is carried out on a regular basis so that you are sufficiently skilled in the exercise that it will have the desired effect when needed. It is no good leaving it until you are highly stressed to begin Progressive Relaxation – IT WON'T WORK.

- As you become more competent with this skill you will also need to address your thoughts. When you relax your mind may wander and it is important that you control your thoughts as they can undo the relaxed state you have acquired. Therefore, once you are relaxed, try to imagine that you are in one of your favourite places. This could be on a beach, in the countryside, by a stream or whatever. By concentrating on this location and recalling how happy you have been there, it will prevent the mind from thinking the things that are worrying you.

- Deep breathing exercises and meditation are also particularly good for relaxation. When we are stressed our breathing becomes rapid and high in our chests. If we can master breathing slowly and from the abdomen it has a calming effect and we will be able to utilise this skill as soon as our stress levels begin to rise. This can be accomplished by meditation which slows down the heart and respiratory rate and decreases blood pressure. One of the most basic methods is as follows:

Find a quiet space where you will not be disturbed and practice the following exercise for several minutes each day:

1) Assume a comfortable posture lying on your back or sitting.
2) If you are sitting, keep the spine straight and let your shoulders drop.
3) Close your eyes if it feels comfortable.
4) Focus your attention on your stomach, feeling it rise on breathing in and fall on breathing out.
5) Concentrate on your breathing, actually 'being' with each breath.
6) Every time you notice that your mind has wandered off the breath, notice what it was that took your concentration away, and then gently bring your attention back to your stomach and the feeling of the breath coming in and out.

7) If your mind wanders away from the breath, then your task is to simply bring it back to the breath every time, no matter what it has become preoccupied with.

Practice this exercise for fifteen minutes, at a convenient time every day, whether you feel like it or not, for one week – and see how it feels to incorporate a disciplined meditation practice into your life. Be aware of how it feels to spend time each day just being with your breath, being 'in the moment' without having to do anything.

A different set of techniques which may help concentrate on changing the way we think. Let us briefly return to our definition of stress. Stress, we have said, occurs when we feel that we cannot cope with a situation. It follows, therefore, that if we can learn to change our perception of the situation, our brain will not trigger a stress response. Our perception of the situation allowed the stress response to happen. Therefore, we have the power to stop it.

- **We must appraise situations differently**
  The key must lie in changing the way we view situations and learning to prevent ourselves from allowing our imaginations to run riot and become our own worst enemies. We all have days when we can only see the bad side of things. It may start in the morning with thinking we look awful/our hair is a mess, and progress to feelings of incompetence by lunchtime and perhaps culminate with the view that friends are not being supportive. When we are highly stressed like this our thinking tends to become more and more negative and we look only on the black side of things. At such times we waste time mulling over minor problems, convincing ourselves that we will soon be facing major catastrophes. We worry about the stressful situation that may occur, thus making the present situation stressful. We really are our own worst enemies. We need to learn when to tackle annoyances and when to let them go. It is the value that you place on

71

what isn't right that causes you stress. For instance, let us assume that you have had a busy day and have finally managed to sit down and relax in front of the television. You then notice that one of the ornaments on the mantelpiece has been moved slightly so that it is now not exactly displayed to perfection. Some people would see this but decide it can stay as it is until the following day – a sensible decision. Others would immediately get up and move the object, thereby using up more energy and effort and further increasing their stress levels. Another example is where someone who is rushing to leave the house to go to work will stop to straighten the bath mat or towel because they spot that it isn't at ninety degrees to the tiles and therefore looks untidy. We all have these foibles and they are totally harmless as long as we know when to ignore them and thus conserve our energy for more important issues.

Ask yourself, 'Are my thoughts logical? Is there evidence for my way of thinking? Would family or friends agree with my view? If a friend did the same thing, would I be as critical as I am or myself?'

Society has taught us that mistakes are bad. Very few people make mistakes and actually consider whether they have learned anything from the experience. Rather they come away feeling a failure. I am certainly not known for my culinary skills and when something I cook doesn't turn out right I automatically attribute it to my uselessness at cooking. It would be unjust to lay the blame for my distress on the cookery disaster, as the distress has resulted from my self-criticism, i.e. my inner voice. It is important to recognise that we learn by making mistakes. When you learn to ride a bike you begin by falling off. Each time this happens you learn a little more about the skills needed to maintain your balance and propel the bike until you master the technique. If we could harness this way of perceiving mistakes into all other aspects of our lives we would reduce a significant amount of our stress. A re-thinking approach is called for. You must learn to recognise when your mood is being determined by negative thinking. At first you will probably only realise it has happened after the event, but, eventually you will be sensitive to the time it is actually occurring and will therefore be in a position to stop it and adopt a more realistic attitude. In turn this will make you a more resilient individual.

- **Boost your self esteem**
  As Eleanor Roosevelt once said, 'No one can make you feel inferior without your consent.' Self-esteem and self-efficacy are central to the sustained success of any individual as they provide a potent vaccine against stress, depression and helplessness. It is important, therefore that we consider ways of building up our levels of self-esteem. Let us begin by considering how we decide if we are 'OK' or whether we are one of life's failures. We tend to base our worthiness on the following:
  a) Our achievements.
  b) The quality of our relationships – this tells us whether others find us acceptable and want to be in our company.
  c) Owning assets.
  d) Possessing good physical characteristics (although few of us seem to be happy with our bodies).
  e) Having competency in significant areas.
  f) Being a good partner/parent/friend.
  g) Being loved.
  h) Being approved of.

The trouble with measuring our worth in this manner is that it diminishes as we find ourselves wanting in one or more of the above factors. For example, if we judge ourselves on how much we are loved and then our partner leaves us, our self-esteem plummets. It would be far better if we could judge ourselves on the positive side of our lives and learn self-acceptance. We are all fallible. We all have faults. We need to accept ourselves for what we are, warts and all. If you want to make changes in your life, or want to achieve your ambitions and dreams, you must first of all believe in yourself. After all, if you don't, why should anyone else. Look at the following situations and typical responses. Can your responses be more likened to those in column A or B?

You can see from the two different types of responses how our state of mind will affect our reactions to events. If we learn to take a more positive approach to life it will help us to minimise our body's stress reactions. Whilst we have no control over what has already happened in our lives, we have the ability to change how we feel. The following are examples of the ways in which we can change our perceptions and simultaneously build our self-confidence.

Change your Self Talk

Many people have learned to be self-deprecating. Maybe as children they were constantly told they were 'not good enough' or compared unfavourably with other children; as adults they may have been constantly 'put down' by others until all of their confidence disappeared. When this happens our internal dialogue becomes negative. Test this out for yourself. Over the next few days, note down both the positive and negative thoughts you have about yourself starting as soon as you wake up in the morning until you go to bed at night. You may be surprised when you examine the list. Try to introduce more positive thoughts into each day. Start the morning, for instance, by telling yourself that you are going to have a great day. You look good etc. If you do this seriously for even a short time you will slowly begin to believe what you are telling yourself. Next, you need to view what you see as your shortcomings in a different light. If, for example, you see yourself as being sensitive, then try to change that perception to being thoughtful and unselfish. If you are intolerant, see yourself as being truthful and law abiding instead. If you think that you are irresponsible then perhaps you need to see yourself as being full

Situation	Column A Typical mental monologue	Column B Constructive self-talk alternative
Difficulty with a doctor/ consultant/ professional	'I hate that person.' 'S/he makes me feel stupid.' 'We'll never get along.'	'I don't feel comfortable with him/her and I need to discover why this is.' 'I let myself get on edge when he's around.' 'It will take some effort to get along but we'll get there.'
Flat tyre on the way to hospital appointment	'Damn this old car.' (Paces around car, looking at flat tyre.) 'We'll miss the appointment and then we'll wait ages for a new one.'	'Bad time for a flat but at least it didn't cause an accident.' I'll call the hospital and explain we are running late.' This shouldn't take long to sort out. Luckily the sun is shining.'

of fun; try to change being pessimistic to being sensible and reliable and finally try to see being obsessive as meticulous.

b) RELATIONSHIPS WITH PROFESSIONALS

The survey showed that parents are not always satisfied with their relationships with the professionals involved in caring for their children. In some cases they were unhappy with the way in which information was given to them but, in most, it was because they were not given (enough) information when they needed it. Additionally, parents thought that the professionals did not listen to them or, if they did listen, little action followed.

The parents cannot directly change the attitude and behaviour of those professionals who are causing the problems. They can, however, learn to become more confident and assertive. These skills will help them to communicate more effectively and obtain answers to their questions.

Learn to be Assertive

Assertive behaviour is a tool to satisfy the needs and wants of all parties that are involved in a situation and will help to make people take you seriously. Because of this, if at all possible, it is best not to give way to emotional extremes of any kind as this could undermine your efforts. Remaining calm can only help your cause.

Become aware of the body language you are conveying. Look directly at the person you are speaking to (without staring, which may make them feel threatened). If you look down or away too much, they may think you are not paying attention or are not sure about what you want. Try to adopt an open posture, in other words, oriented towards the person you are speaking to and not crossing arms or legs. When standing, always try to face the person directly and avoid standing to the side. Hold your position and do not back away.

As a parent or carer you will almost always put other people's needs before your own. To be assertive it helps to know your rights and theirs, and to take an active part in decisions made about your child and his/her future.

Think about what your rights are and make a list of them according to your own situation. It will include:
- I have a right to fully understand.
- I have the right to be involved.

- I have the right to speak.
- I have the right to be heard.
- I have the right to state my feelings (frustrated, hopeful etc.)
- I have the right to be respected.
- We have the right to be treated with dignity.

The people you are dealing with will also come from the standpoint of their own rights, and listening to these will help in resolving issues.

Some do's and don'ts:

- Do understand what you are feeling.
- Do state your feelings and your needs. For example, I am feeling frustrated because I am not sure that you are the person I need to speak to about this problem. Please confirm the situation for me.
- Do tell the person you are communicating with what you want.
- Do not make assumptions.
- Do make sure you are asking for things that are obtainable. You may need to ask someone else.
- Do stick to your objectives. If you need to, practice first or write things down.
- Do not be afraid to refer to what you have written down.
- Do be clear in your mind that to be assertive is different to being aggressive. Signs of aggression are shouting, not allowing the other person to speak, or not realising that they may have problems and rights too.
- Do respect others' rights simultaneously with your own.

In order to prepare to be assertive you may need to begin to think in a slightly different way. It is not always easy to make personal changes, especially when you are under pressure. It will almost certainly be worthwhile to take time to rehearse the potential situation and prepare by writing down a list of things you will need to know:

- WHO is the other person involved?
- WHEN will this take place?
- HOW will you deal with this?
- WHAT FEAR do you have if you become assertive?
- WHAT is your behaviour GOAL?

For example:

I have regular appointments with doctors. They never explain the potential side effects of the medication they prescribe for my child. We discover the effects through trial and error. I find this upsetting and frustrating.

Breaking down the situation may look something like this:

I have an appointment with my GP (who). I usually need to see him after paediatric appointments (when). It would prepare me if he explained that side effects were likely when my child's medication is changed (how). If I ask him he may think I am stepping into his territory (fear). I would like to be better informed (goal).

Try a six-step plan to complete the changes:

1. **Find out what you have a right to ask for.**

   Is this a right or a request? Sometimes, something that you think is a moral right will not be a legal one. Be sure of your ground.

2. **Allow time to discuss your needs.**

   Make sure the appointment time allows for this discussion. If not, perhaps you could make better arrangements to discuss the matter.

3. **Speak to the person concerned. If you speak to the wrong person they may not be able to help.**

   Tell them directly what the problem is. They could be unaware that they are creating a problem. For example, I am having trouble with the medical terms. I am not familiar with them.

4. Tell them how you feel about it.

When you express your feelings you are letting the other person know the results of their actions. They may be stimulating your feelings, but ultimately only you have control over what you feel, for example, I feel frustrated when you speak as if you are not listening to me.

5. Ask for what you want.

Asking is the key. Remember to use assertive body language. Keep it simple. Ask for one thing at a time. Be specific. I have listened to you. I would like it if you would listen to me now. Stay calm. Do not apologise. Think of the behaviour as the problem, not the person; speaking about the behaviour instead, preserves respect. Ask for what you want, do not demand.

6. Tell this person the consequences.

It is better that we both listen to each other in order that we may reach agreement with the minimum of fuss.

Whilst these assertiveness skills are developing, there may still be an occasion or two where you become angry with the person you are talking to. This can only have negative results and it gives the other person 'the moral high ground'.

Therefore it is very important that you learn to manage your anger.

To manage anger you must first of all analyse the situations which cause you to become angry, eg. what is it about the person who is making you angry? What triggers your anger? And then you must examine your feelings. Why are you angry? Are you being fair? Are you in control? Learn to develop relaxation skills as they will help you to remain in control at all times.

c) ISSUES RELATING TO FAMILY AND FRIENDS

Parents often feel guilty because they do not always spend sufficient time with other family members. Whilst recognising that caring for a disabled child is a full-time role, it is worth looking at your time management skills as every minute saved is time gained to ease your conscience and thereby reduce your level of stress.

• **Learn to Manage your Time**

Crisis management will often give us a buzz of excitement and in the short term it will do us no harm. Long term, however, it will impact on our health, private/social lives and could prove fatal.

Most of us feel that there are not enough hours in the day but few of us will actually invest twenty minutes or so to analyse our normal practices and to determine ways of becoming more efficient. We must achieve our desired effect with minimum waste or effort and do so as naturally and easily as possible.

Time Management skills allow you to plan efficiently and effectively and to allocate the amount of time according to the importance of the task. In other words, you will be more in control of what you do which will lead to you being more productive and thereby having more time to relax and enjoy your leisure time.

Time management is being able to control the time you have to ensure that you afford time to the things in life that you say you value. What do you value most of all? Your health, your family or friends. Nearly everyone will say that their health is of utmost importance. Yet, when asked how much time is devoted to health it is very low. In other words, we say we value our health and well-being but actually do very little to foster same. Ironically it is only when we become ill that we suddenly turn all of our attention to our health, but this is the wrong approach. We must learn to be proactive and not reactive. We must learn to manage our time so that we can enjoy all three factors, namely our health, family and friends. Caring for a disabled child doesn't leave much free time, but if you have no leisure time and become ill, who looks after the child then?

Rules for Managing Time

1) List the tasks for the day or week.
2) Break each job into chunks as each completed section will provide motivation to continue.
3) Do not let the list become your master.
4) Think carefully before agreeing to undertake extra work/ tasks/favours.
5) Do not procrastinate. We all have jobs we hate doing but they become even more stressful if they are left until last.
6) Get rid of any routine you have found yourself in if you consider it to be a waste of time.
7) Plan ahead and do not plan too many changes at once. Also, try to plan for changes to occur when other things in your life will be least stressful.
8) Remember, it is your life. Time management will help you to feel in control.

Parents are also stressed by the hurtful comments and criticisms made by family members and friends. You must try to surround yourself with positive influences as these will support you. After all, if you surround yourself with people who are cynical and bitter about things, it is going to be very difficult for you to maintain your positive perspective. Negative people can very quickly have a damaging effect on others so try to mix with friends who have a positive outlook on life as they will nurture your good feelings and help you.

And remember, unless the criticism is constructive in nature, do not accept it. You have no control over what other people will say to you but you do not need to internalise the message. Do not give it any of your time. If someone doesn't like the way you are doing something, it is his/ her problem, not yours.

Enjoy the company of those who make you laugh and help you to relax. Avoid those who make you feel uneasy and prevent you from enjoying your leisure time – it is too precious to waste on those who annoy or depress you. Some people will be difficult to get on with, but it is important to try and handle it as professionally as possible.

One of the best ways to feel good about yourself is to be kind and do good deeds for others. Altruism is a common trait in those individuals with positive self-esteem. If you can help to make someone else feel good, it will make you feel good – if this wasn't true, there would be very few voluntary workers in the world. Perhaps this is best illustrated by the following poem.

SMILE

It costs nothing, but means much.

It enriches those who receive it without impoverishing those who give it.

It happens in a flash but the memory sometimes lasts forever.

None are so rich that they can go along without it.

None are so poor that they are not richer for its benefits.

It is rest to the weary,

Daylight to the discouraged,

Sunshine to the sad,

And its nature's best antidote in time of trouble.

Yet it cannot be bought or borrowed or stolen.

For it is something that is no earthly use to anyone

Unless it is given away,

And if in the rush of life or business you see someone too tired to give you a smile;

then leave one of yours;

For no one needs a smile so much as those who have none left to give.

Anon.

- **Recognise your Sources of Support**

  Our social networks can help by acting as a buffer provided we turn to the most appropriate person. Do you turn to the same person regardless of the problem? If so, then you are probably deluding yourself that s/he is helping when, in reality, they are only acting as a sounding board and, in some cases, may be making your stress levels worse as they allow you to spend more and more time going over the same ground, – possibly even encouraging you to do so by sympathising – when what is needed is someone who can either provide practical advice on alleviating your stress or helping to move you on and to stop you dwelling on the situation.

  It must be remembered that everything that happens to us will affect our behaviour in different situations. High levels of stress resulting from a particularly difficult day in the role of carer can put pressure on the family, i.e. the very individuals we are relying on for support. Effective communication is therefore of paramount importance.

  Let us not forget, at this point, the detrimental effect that stress can have on your partner or closest friend who is probably the one who will bear the brunt of your bad moods. It is vital that you make every effort to maintain a good relationship with your nearest and dearest and s/he will be the one who can give you maximum support.

  It is very important that each partner recognises the other's signs and symptoms of stress as he/she will then be in a better position to help. They will realise that the partner is not trying to be difficult, but is acting out of character because s/he has lost their perspective due to stress. Should you detect these signs then choose a moment when you think your partner would be willing to discuss the apparent problem. Point out your concern and explain that you are worried about them. Accusing them of 'letting things slide' because they haven't done the shopping/ cooking/gardening etc. will appear only as a selfish demand that they look after you better.

If you are the one trying to help your partner, it is of paramount importance that you remain calm and rational and do not allow the stress to 'spread' to you. Refuse to get drawn into pointless rows and arguments as this behaviour will only serve to justify your partner's anger. It is the latter which is causing the problem and therefore it is this that needs to be exposed. It is all too easy to argue with a person because you think that they are being illogical, but this solves nothing. The problems will be exacerbated. Instead practice whatever methods of relaxation you have decided to use. It also helps to give yourself time and space on your own.

d) CHILD-CENTRED ISSUES

Parents become highly stressed when they cannot tell if their child is happy and free from pain, due to communication problems resulting from their disability. Likewise, administering medicines and/or lifting and handling the child causes more stress if the parents think they are inflicting further pain and discomfort on their child in their attempt to make them more comfortable. Parents also have to face the dilemma of deciding upon the amount of parental care to maximise the child's safety whilst being conscious of over-protecting their offspring and limiting their freedom and, with it, their opportunity to enjoy life. Those who have never experienced the level of responsibility that carers have to shoulder will find it difficult to fully empathise with the self-doubt that they have to shoulder.

The following commandments for parents/carers may help:

1. Have faith in your ability.
2. Remember that you do not have control over the future – only today. Therefore, take one day at a time.

3. Stop feeling guilty. Remember that just because you spend more time with your disabled child, it doesn't mean that you love your partner/spouse and other children less.

4. Be positive. Concentrate on the good things that happen each day and the joys and pleasure that your child brings.

5. Be honest with yourself. You are human. You are allowed to feel angry, frustrated, upset etc. You cannot always be a supermum or superdad.

6. You do not have to justify yourself to others. Answer to yourself. You know you are doing your best and no-one could ask for more.

7. View life as challenges to seek, not obstacles to avoid.

8. Learn and practice relaxation techniques and look after yourself properly.

9. Your sense of humour is an important muscle in controlling your level of well-being. Exercise it,
and

10. Stop worrying.

e) LEVEL OF SUPPORT

Many parents find it very difficult to obtain information on the types of support that are available and how they can apply for that help. Chapter 8 will provide a lot of this information. However, the aim of parents, generally, should be to empower themselves in order that they can fulfil their roles as carers as effectively as possible.

An empowered parent:
a) knows the rights of his/her child and knows the channels to use to seek justice for his/her child;
b) can contribute to the resolution of the problems the child faces and will not just take instruction from professionals, being afraid to air their views;

c) insists his/her child is included in family and community life and will explore laws and policies to find out how they can protect their son/daughter, and

d) understands and insists that a child with a disability deserves the same dignity as another child.

The more knowledge and information the parents have, the easier it becomes to cope with the 'system'.

In addition to the usual sources of information such as libraries and the Internet, support groups can be a valuable source of help, advice and information. They provide an opportunity for parents to talk to others who are in a similar position, i.e. others who are experiencing or have experienced the same problems. Cerebra is always willing to put parents in contact with organisations with the appropriate expertise needed to help.

f) THE EMPLOYERS

The survey shows that only a small proportion of parents caring for a disabled child are in full-time employment. However, from that small number, some are experiencing extreme stress because of the apparent lack of understanding by the employer, particularly on the occasions when the child is very poorly.

Employers will understandably be anxious to maximise their outputs/profits and often fail to make allowances for the unpredictable nature of the child's needs.

There are employment laws to protect parent/carers from discrimination at work and it is often better for the parent to ask their trade union, support group and/or charitable organisation who have the necessary expertise to deal with the matter on their behalf.

g) PRACTICAL PROBLEMS

The next chapter offers advice on the help that is available to deal with the practical problems parents experience in caring for a disabled child.

BUT REMEMBER – if you try to practice the stress busters already discussed, you will be more able to cope with difficult situations.

STRESS BUSTERS

Learn a Relaxation Technique

Use your Time more Effectively

Learn to be Assertive

Recognise your Signs and Symptoms of Stress
and act accordingly

Know your Rights

Take Regular Physical Exercise

Lead a Healthy Life

Be Positive

CHAPTER 8

FINDING AND USING
INFORMATION

Whilst every care has been taken to ensure that all information contained in this chapter was correct at the time of printing, some of the information may now be out of date. If you wish to make sure that you are being referred to the most recent up to date information, please telephone Cerebra's help line on free phone 0800 32 81 159.

SECTION A – WELFARE BENEFITS

It would be impossible to provide precise and up-to-date information on the types of benefits and allowances you may be entitled to claim as the details are continually changing. However, this chapter will give brief descriptions of the main sources of help, and details of how you should go about applying for each.

NB: If you have any difficulties obtaining the information you require, please do not hesitate to contact Cerebra who are always willing to help.

This section will focus on welfare benefits available to children with a disability and their parents or carers. Your right to some benefits will depend on the effect of your child's disability. Your right to other benefits will depend on your own financial circumstances.

a) DISABILITY LIVING ALLOWANCE (DLA) FOR A CHILD UNDER 16

You can claim DLA for a child with a severe physical or mental illness or disability if they need more help or looking after than other children of the same age because of their illness or disability. Having a child with disabilities may create all sorts of additional expenses. DLA can meet these expenses though you can spend DLA on anything. DLA is not means tested so it doesn't matter if you have savings, are employed or unemployed, have a partner or not. This means how much you have in savings or other income is not taken into account. It is paid on top of other benefits. It is also tax-free. It may help you to claim extra elements in Working Tax Credit or Child Tax Credit. It also may entitle you to an extra premium on means tested benefits like Income Support. Your child also does not need to be registered disabled to apply.

The current rate for DLA can be found on the DWP website www/dwp.gov.uk and you can also download the application form from here.

b) CARER'S ALLOWANCE (CA)
FORMERLY INVALID CARE ALLOWANCE

If the child you care for gets the middle or higher rate of the DLA care component and you care for the child at least thirty-five hours a week, you are eligible for the Carers Allowance (CA). CA is a weekly benefit for anyone looking after a severely disabled person. There are conditions that you must meet to receive this allowance. This is a taxable benefit. You can download an application form for CA from the DWP website or request one by phoning the CA Unit (01253 856 123). In Northern Ireland, contact the Social Security Agency.

Useful websites
CA application form
www.dwp.gov.uk/lifeevent/benefits/carers_allowance.htm#download
Social Security Agency www.ssani.gov.uk/gbi/benefits/CA.htm
State Pension www.thepensionservice.gov.uk/pdf/PM9_nov2002.pdf
DWP website www.dwp.gov.uk

c) TAX CREDITS (CHILD TAX CREDIT, WORKING TAX CREDIT)

You will qualify for Child Tax Credit (CTC) if you have at least one dependent child and your income is sufficiently low. It is estimated that nine out of ten families are eligible for Child Tax Credit so it is worth claiming.

There are two parts to CTC. There is the child element that includes an amount for each child. You will get a disability element for any child in your family who gets DLA. You will also get a severe disability element for each child who gets the highest rate of the care component of DLA.

There is a family element that includes an amount for each family and an additional amount for any baby under one in the family.

Working Tax Credit is paid to top up your earnings if you are working for at least sixteen hours a week and expect to work for at least four weeks. It includes help with the costs of childcare. You can be eligible for up to 70% of the cost of registered childcare. This can include childcare in your own home if the carer is a childminder.

Whenever you put in your claim, your award will be calculated to the following April. You have to make a new claim each year. Payments for the child are paid direct to the main carer for the child. Couples must make a joint application for one tax credit. Both are administered by the Inland Revenue, their Helpline number is 0845 300 3900.

Useful website
Inland revenue
https://www.taxcredits.inlandrevenue.gov.uk/HomeIR.aspx

d) INCOME SUPPORT, JOBSEEKER'S ALLOWANCE AND OTHER BENEFITS FOR THOSE WITH A LOW INCOME

Income Support (IS)
This benefit can be paid to lone parents, carers, people who are incapable of work, or people aged sixty and over.

If you do not fit into these categories, you will have to sign on for employment and claim income-based Jobseeker's Allowance instead.

Income-based Jobseeker's Allowance
This benefit is for people under pension age who are required to be available for work.

Both Income support and Income-based Jobseeker's Allowance are benefits for people working less than sixteen hours a week and have a low income.

The amount of savings will affect the amount of benefit you will get. Other benefits such as 'Child Benefit' and 'Carers Allowance' will be treated as income but DLA will not. If you own your own home, Income Support and Income-based Jobseeker's Allowance can also help with mortgage costs and are the only benefits that do so. You can claim either of these benefits at your local Jobcentre Plus office.

Social Fund
This is a fund that makes payments to people in need. It makes regulated payments such as Sure Start Maternity Grants, funeral

expense payments, cold weather payments, and winter fuel payments. It is administered by DWP.

Sure Start Maternity Grant
This is a payment of up to £500 that can be claimed if you have recently had, or are expecting, a baby. It can be claimed if you receive Income Support or Income-based Jobseeker's Allowance, child tax credit above the family element, or Working Tax Credit which includes the element for a disabled worker.

Funeral Expense Payments
This can be claimed if you are responsible for arranging a funeral and you receive one of the benefits listed for the Sure Start grant, housing or council tax benefit.

Cold Weather Payments
Extra payments made if there is a spell of very cold weather. These payments are automatic if you claim Income Support or Income-based Jobseeker's Allowance and have children under five, someone in the family who is sick and disabled, or are over sixty.

Winter Fuel Payment
A one-off payment is made to help those over the age of sixty with their winter heating bills.

Discretionary Grants and Loans from the Social Fund
The Discretionary Social Fund makes Community Care Grants that don't need to be repaid, and Budgeting Loans and Crisis Loans that do need to be repaid. These payments are strictly budget limited.

Community Care Grants
These are made to help people live independently in the community. It might be for furniture or kitchen equipment or items needed because of a disability. It also can help with fares to

visit your child in hospital and may include overnight accommodation. You apply on Form SF300 available from the local DWP office or Jobcentre Plus office. If you have a disabled child, you should be able to claim a grant rather than a loan. It is often worth asking for a review of a Community Care Grant as the DWP office has a certain amount of money each month and they may have more money in their budget when your claim is reviewed.

Budgeting Loans

These are made for items such as furniture and household equipment, clothing and footwear, rent in advance, and travelling expenses. You must have the ability to repay the loan from your existing benefits. To apply you will need to obtain the Form SF300.

Crisis Loans

These are designed to meet emergency expenses. You can apply using Form SF401 or by calling at your local DWP office or Jobcentre Plus office. The loan must be the only means of preventing serious damage or serious risk to the health or safety of the householder or a member of their family. The emergency may be loss of money, or a hardship as your regular income is in arrears, or a disaster like a fire or flood has occurred.

Housing Benefit (HB) and Council Tax Benefit (CTB)

If your income is low and you pay rent or pay council tax, you can apply for Housing Benefit and Council Tax Benefit from your local authority if you live in England or Wales. (In Northern Ireland, you can get help through HB towards Domestic Rates. There is no council tax). In determining your income, both earnings and benefits are taken into account. If you receive either Income Support or Income-based Jobseeker's Allowance, you should qualify for full HB and CTB.

Useful websites

Income Support

http://www.dwp.gov.uk/lifeevent/benefits/income_support.asp

Income-based Jobseeker's Allowance

http://www.jobcentreplus.gov.uk/cms.asp?Page=/Home/Customers/WorkingAgeBenefits/497

Social Fund

Sure Start Maternity Grant

www.dwp.gov.uk/publications/dwp/2002/maternity/index.asp

Funeral Expense payments

http://www.jobcentreplus.gov.uk/cms.asp?Page=/Home/Customers/WorkingAgeBenefits/1029

Cold Weather payments

http://www.jobcentreplus.gov.uk/cms.asp?Page=/Home/Customers/WorkingAgeBenefits/485

Winter Fuel payments www.thepensionservice.gov.uk/winterfuel/

Community Care Grants

www.dwp.gov.uk/lifeevent/benefits/community_care_grants.asp

Budgeting Loans

http://www.jobcentreplus.gov.uk/cms.asp?Page=/Home/Customers/WorkingAgeBenefits/1008

Crisis Loans www.dwp.gov.uk/lifeevent/benefits/crisis_loans.asp

Housing Benefit

www.dwp.gov.uk/lifeevent/benefits/housing_benefit.asp

Council Tax Benefit

www.dwp.gov.uk/lifeevent/benefits/council_tax_benefit.asp

e) HEALTH BENEFITS

If you receive Income Support, receive Working Tax Credit with Child Tax Credit (CTC), and meet the income requirements, or are named on a Tax Credit NHS Exemption Certificate, you can receive help with health costs including:

• Free NHS prescriptions

- Free NHS dental treatment
- Free NHS sight tests
- Vouchers toward the cost of glasses and contact lenses
- Repayment of necessary travel costs to hospital and back for NHS treatment

Useful website
www.dwp.gov.uk/lifeevent/benefits/help_with_health_costs.asp

f) OTHER BENEFITS AVAILABLE

Exemption from Vehicle Excise Duty
If your child receives the higher rate of the mobility component of DLA, you can claim exemption from Road Tax. You can request Form DLA 403 (or MLS303 in Northern Ireland) from the Benefits Enquiry Line Freephone 0800 882200 (0800 220674 in Northern Ireland).

Free School Meals
Children are entitled to free school lunches if the parent(s) receive(s) Income Support or Child Tax Credit (CTC) but not Working Tax Credit, and the CTC is paid at the maximum rate.

Council Tax Reduction
If your home has been specially adapted for your disabled son or daughter, the council tax may be reduced to that of a property in the band immediately below yours. These adaptations may include an extra room needed for the child with disabilities or space so a wheelchair may be used inside. The person liable for council tax must make the application.

Child Benefit
You can claim Child Benefit if you are responsible for a child under sixteen or a child under the age of nineteen who is in full-time, non-advanced education. This benefit is tax-free and

is not means tested. It also does not matter if your child is home or away. The 'Inland Revenue' is responsible for this benefit. You can download a claim form from their website and you can also make a claim on-line. You can also report a change in circumstances on-line.

Useful Websites
Child Benefit
http://www.dwp.gov.uk/childbenefit/
Inland Revenue
www.inlandrevenue.gov.uk/childbenefit/eligible.htm

g) IMPROVING A HOME

Disabled Facilities Grant
Mandatory grants are awarded after an occupational therapist from social services has assessed whether adaptations proposed are necessary and appropriate. Grants are available to make it easier for your child with a disability to get into and around your home or to provide suitably adapted bathroom facilities, heating and controls. There has been a campaign to stop means testing for this grant. This has been successful in Northern Ireland and is changing in the autumn 2005 in Wales. England and Scotland are still debating this issue as we go to press.

The council has discretion to give grants for a wide range of other works to make a home suitable for a disabled occupant's accommodation, welfare or employment needs. The council will be able to advise you further about these possibilities. Contact your Housing Grant Department at your Local Authority.

Home Insulation Grants
If your child gets DLA, or you get WTC or CTC, you will be eligible to receive a grant towards insulating and draught-proofing your home. Freephone 0800 0720150.

Useful Website
Disabled Facilities Grant
http://www.odpm.gov.uk/stellent/groups/odpm_housing/documents/
page/odpm_house_602543.hcsp

h) SUPPORT

There are many avenues for parents/carers to get advice and advocacy support. The Benefits Enquiry Line has a Freephone number 0800 88200 and gives general advice and information on all benefits for both disabled persons and carers. For specific questions about DLA, there is a special Helpline 0845 7123456 and they may have access to your records. A local source of information is '**Citizens Advice**' (formerly the '**Citizens Advice Bureau**'). There may be a Disability Rights organisation in your area. They will provide benefits information and some provide an advocacy service. Many are linked to '**Disability Information Advice Line**' (DIAL) contactable on 01302 310123.

Two comprehensive books on welfare benefits are published by the '**Disability Alliance**' (Disability Rights Handbook £9.50 for individuals on benefit) and the '**Child Poverty Action Group**' (Welfare Benefits and Tax Credits Handbook at a cost of £8.80 to individuals).

Useful Websites
Citizens Advice Bureau
www.nacab.org.uk
DIAL (Disability Information Advice Line)
www.dialuk.org.uk
Disability Alliance
www.disabilityalliance.org
Child Poverty Action Group
www.cpag.org.uk
Department for Works and Pensions
www.dwp.gov.uk

Social Security Agency Northern Ireland
www.ssani.gov.uk
Inland Revenue Tax Credits
https://www.taxcredits.inlandrevenue.gov.uk/HomeIR.aspx
Disability Living Allowance (DLA) for a child under sixteen
– Download an application
http://www.dwp.gov.uk/lifeevent/benefits/disability_liv_allowance2.asp
Cerebra
Download DLA Guide www.cerebra.org.uk/dla1new.pdf
Request info@cerebra.org.uk
Motability
www.motability.co.uk
DWP website
www.dwp.gov.uk

SECTION B – WELFARE SERVICES

This section describes some other welfare and care services
that are available, mostly through government and voluntary
organisations.

a) SOCIAL SERVICES

Assessments
If your child is disabled, you may need extra help or support.
You can contact the Social Services Department in your Local
Authority. You should be able to find their contact details by
looking in a phone book under the name of your County
Borough, Borough Council or, in some areas, new Unitary
Authority, or London Borough. If you live in Scotland, look
under the name of your Regional or Island Council.

Local authorities differ in the services they provide. If you
ask, a local council should send you a document outlining the
services they provide and how to access them. Before social

services provide any service for your family, they will want to know more about your child and the family. This is called an '**assessment**'. You can request an assessment, or alternatively can be referred by a '**GP**' or '**health visitor**'. The assessment will usually be carried out by a social worker and involve the child where possible. The information collected will be discussed with the parents and will be confidential.

An assessment may look at things like:
• aids the child may need,
• adaptations to the home,
• respite care,
• any particular care needs,
• whether the needs are likely to change.

It is a good idea to think what you would like and why you need it before the assessment takes place. Writing things down will help you remember everything you want to mention.

The assessment will help produce a care plan for your child saying what service will be provided. If you are not given a written copy, you should request it. This care plan should be reviewed at intervals and should not be changed without a re-assessment of the child's needs.

The Local Authority has a duty to provide services for disabled children to minimise the effects of their disability. They may provide:
• respite care,
• home help,
• help with a holiday, and
• after school care for school-age children.

The services they will provide vary between local authorities. Instead of providing services, the local authority may offer 'Direct Payments'.

The range of further information on direct payments and how to apply for them, can be easily accessed from the Department of Health Website.

b) CARER'S ASSESSMENT

The Carers and Disabled Children Act (England and Wales) covers:

- Carers (aged sixteen or over) who provide a substantial amount of care on a regular basis for someone aged eighteen or over, and
- People with parental responsibility for a disabled child who provide a substantial amount of care on a regular basis for the child.

The purpose of the Act is to support people who choose to remain in their caring roles and to help them maintain their own health and well being.

This Act provides the right to a carer's assessment even where the person cared for has refused an assessment for community care services or refused the services themselves. The Act also provides social services with the power to supply certain services direct to carers following assessment.

If you look after a disabled child who needs support to live at home, your local Social Services department may be able to make things easier for you. As well as providing services to the one you care for, they may be able to provide services for you as a carer.

Your needs will be considered as part of an assessment of needs of your child and family. It gives you an opportunity to tell Social Services about things that could make caring easier for you. For example:

- Are you getting enough sleep?
- Do you get any time for yourself and can you get out and about?
- Other things you may be spending more time on, even without noticing, and that may add up to make a difference, including bathing, toileting, dressing, dealing with incontinence and other needs, organising things, medication and treatment, dealing with feeding difficulties or special diets.

A range of services is available to help and support carers to enable them to continue in their caring role. This might include help in the home, help with transport, home visiting and possibly organising short breaks (which is normally termed respite care) to allow carers to 'recharge their batteries'.

The 'Care Manager' is normally the person who comes to make the assessment. Your care manager will be able to describe to you what your options are and what services are available locally.

Direct payments may be made to carers (including sixteen and seventeen year old carers) to meet their own assessed needs, and to parents of a disabled child so that they may meet the assessed needs of both the disabled child and the family.

c) RESPITE

Respite is a word that simply means having a rest or taking a break from your normal routine. For parents of a child/children with disabilities, getting a rest from the day-to-day caring responsibilities can be very difficult. This need is recognised and local authorities have developed schemes to provide respite for parents and carers. Some authorities have special homes where the child can go with varied activities provided. This gives both the parents and siblings a rest too. Some Social Services provide a respite service where approved child-minders can watch the children at either their own home or at the childminder's home, and allow the parents a night out.

There is now an emphasis in giving parents and children more choice in all parts of the UK, and Social Services have developed a more flexible approach and a greater range of short-term breaks. Other local Social Services have formed partnerships with voluntary organisations who provide the respite service. There is also the possibility of using Direct Payments to give the family the best choice of the break they would want.

The UK Government had made money available to local authorities via the Carers Grant to set up local schemes to provide breaks for carers. In England and Northern Ireland, many local authorities have set up a voucher system. They provide vouchers to carers who can redeem them at approved leisure schemes or respite homes. Families may need to meet some extra costs. Because the Government grants for the schemes are fixed, vouchers are distributed according to assessed need by Social Services. Some councils have used the grants to fund agencies to provide short term breaks. For example, there may be a holiday club for children and young people with disabilities, or an away weekend for children with a physical disability and challenging behaviour. Check with your local Social Services about the respite services that they offer.

There are also a number of charities that either offer holiday sites at a reduced price, holidays for young people, or grants for holidays. For these, your child does not need to come under a Social Services respite scheme, although grant-makers may ask for a testimonial from a professional who knows the child. The Family Fund is probably the best known in the UK and is the next topic. The Winged Fellowship Trust has five UK centres and provides 7,000 breaks annually for visually impaired and disabled people. The Charity BREAK also provides holidays and respite care for children and families with special needs. Barnardo's and The Children's Society run various projects that provide short-term respite breaks throughout the country. The Cerebra information service can provide a more complete list of providers on request.

Useful websites
Winged Fellowship Trust – www.wft.org.uk
BREAK – www.break-charity.org
Barnardo's – www.barnardos.org.uk
The Children's Society – www.childrensociety.org.uk
Cerebra – www.cerebra.org.uk

Many agencies that provide childminding or play-schemes, especially in the summer, have to be registered with their local Social Services but are not a part of the official respite system. They charge a variety of fees, some quite modest. To find them in England, Scotland and Wales, so far, they are gradually being added to the local lists available from the Children's Information Service, www.childcarelink.gov.uk/index/asp or freephone 08000 960296.

d) THE FAMILY FUND AND THE FAMILY WELFARE ASSOCIATION (FWA)

The Family Fund is a UK-wide organisation funded by the government's administrations of each region. Its purpose is to ease the stress on families who care for severely disabled children under the age of sixteen years, by providing grants and information related to the care of the child.

They consider applications from families with children who have the following conditions: Alimentary conditions, behaviour and emotional conditions, blood disorders, cancers and leukaemia, chromosome disorders, communication difficulties, endocrine, metabolic and storage diseases, epilepsy, foetal and environmental development conditions, heart conditions, immune system conditions, learning disability or difficulty, liver conditions, motor and skeletal disorders, renal disorders, respiratory conditions, skin conditions, undiagnosed and complex conditions.

After considering a child's disability eligibility, the Family Fund has to check that the family's income and savings come within the Fund's financial limits. DLA, Child Benefit and fostering services are not counted but other benefits like Carers Allowance are. Parents are asked to provide details of their finances in their application. All information families provide is confidential.

An application must be submitted and this can be a paper copy or completed on-line at the fund's website www.family-fundtrust.org.uk. If it is the first time a family has applied, it is likely that a local visitor will arrange to call and discuss the request.

Once a family's application is accepted, they can apply for help with the following:

- holidays or leisure activities so everyone in the family can have a break;
- washing machine or tumble dryer because of constant bed-wetting or dirty laundry;
- bedding and clothing to cover the expense of wear and tear because of the child's disability;
- bed if a replacement is needed because of the child's disability;
- driving lessons for the child's main carer, if there is a car available;
- transport expenses if the child does not get the higher rate mobility component of DLA but still has difficulty getting around;
- fridge-freezer if the child's disability makes shopping difficult;
- hospital visiting costs such as long distance journeys for NHS treatment;
- telephone if this is essential for medical or social reasons;
- play equipment if this is related to the child's special needs.

They have publications that can help parents and young disabled people, including a booklet 'After 16 – What's New?' The Fund also maintains a website 'After 16' at www.after16.org.uk

Parents can apply each year as long as they continue to meet the fund's criteria.

Family Welfare Association (FWA)
The FWA is a charity that helps families on low incomes, especially those living on benefits. They provide families with essential items such as beds, cookers and children's shoes. They also help with fuel bills and disability aids.

Applications must be made through referral by a professional person such as a social worker or health visitor, or by a volunteer agency such as Citizens Advice. If funds are available and an application can be accepted, an application form will be sent to the referrer.

If an application is successful, all grant payments are made to the referring agency or service/utilities provider. No cheques are made payable to individuals. Further information is available on www.fwa.org.uk

e) EQUIPMENT

Social Services should provide a range of aids and equipment for children with disabilities to make is easier to manage at home. Once contacted, Social Services will usually arrange for an occupational or physiotherapist visit to make an assessment as to what type of equipment would be best to help the child.

Mobility Aids

If the child has problems with mobility for example, a wheelchair or other walking aid may be required. These are usually loaned to the family, as the child is likely to out-grow whatever equipment is supplied. There may be a local NHS wheelchair service while, in Wales, the Artificial Limb and Appliance Service (ALAS) has two centres that provide this service. They will help you choose from what they have available.

If your child would benefit from a powered indoor/outdoor wheelchair, the wheelchair service may be able to provide one, again subject to an assessment of the child's need. These are expensive items and therefore are probably in short supply. If this is the case, you can approach a number of charities that exist to help children be mobile and more independent. Whizz-Kidz is a charity that helps raise money for disabled children who need mobility aids which cannot be obtained from statutory sources (for example NHS or social services). You can receive information about applying for a mobility aid by phoning 020 7233 6600 or by e-mail to info@whizz-kidz.org.uk Another scheme is the Easy Rider Scheme run by the Variety Club of Great Britain. An application form and guidelines for applicants can be downloaded from their website at www.varietyclub.org.uk The Easy Rider Scheme can apply to children up to the age of nineteen years, but they have a long waiting list so it is advisable to apply before the age of seventeen years.

Other Equipment

There is a wide range of equipment available to help families caring for a child with disabilities. Special communication aids, cutlery, chairs and cushions are a few of these. Throughout the UK there are Disabled Living Centres (DLC) that provide advice, assessment and the opportunity to try out equipment. Services are impartial and are usually free of charge. To find the nearest DLC to you, look at the DLC website at www.dlcc.org.uk/

Nappies and Continence Supplies

Parents should contact their health visitor or doctor about help available and how to apply for continence equipment from the local health service. This could include disposable nappies, bed pads and plastic pants. Provision appears to differ according to where you live, often referred to as a postcode lottery. There often is a specialist continence health visitor who can give advice and will know of any other sources for continence aids in your local area, and help with laundry services. Otherwise further advice is available from ERIC, a voluntary organisation at www.enuresis.org.uk There is also a paid laundry service from Eco-babes at www.eco-babes.co.uk

f) PORTAGE

Portage is a pre-school educational programme for develop-mentally delayed children who have difficulty in learning basic skills. The educational programme usually takes place in the home where parents or carers are responsible for teaching the child daily, with weekly supervisory visits from a Home Advisor. Portage provides practical guidance to parents on the day-to-day care of a child and advice on how to stimulate the child. Portage supports families from the time that any additional needs are first apparent which can be soon after birth or any time in the pre-school period.

Home Advisors are specially trained in understanding child development. They initially assess the child's performance level with motor skills, cognitive skills, language skills, socialisation skills and self-help skills. Then an individualised programme is prepared for the child. Teaching targets are set each week. The Home Advisor demonstrates how to teach each skill to the parents. The Home Advisors also meet regularly with a supervisor and project administrator to report on home visits and to try and find solutions to any problems that have come up.

Portage usually continues until the child is no longer experiencing difficulties or has started school. The Home Advisor has contacts with other professionals and can recommend other helpful services that may be available to the parent and child in their locality. Portage services are in many areas of England and Wales. In Scotland and Northern Ireland there maybe informal sources of portage or early stimulation, and it is worth trying the National Portage Association to find out, telephone 01935 471641 Monday or Thursday 9.00a.m.–1.00p.m. In England or Wales visit www.portage.org.uk/map.html to find out if your area is covered by Portage.

g) SUPPORT ORGANISATIONS

Most parents find themselves in a strange land when they discover one of their children has a disabling condition. Often Health and Social Services do not have the time or there are financial restraints to supporting the parents and family through this new journey.

Many find the best support is from others who are travelling or have travelled the same road before them. For most brain-related conditions, you will find a charity, or volunteer support group, who can give you up-to-date information as well as personal support. Charities like Cerebra and Contact a Family in the UK can point you to an appropriate national, or sometimes local, group for your child's condition. (It is usually possible to find them on the Internet but it is still the case that many organisations are only easily located from directories and databases held by such charities, using the knowledge of the advisors there). Some families have children with undiagnosed conditions and there are support groups for these families too.

Useful websites
Cerebra – www.cerebra.org.uk
Contact a Family – www.cafamily.org.uk

Internet Forums and e-groups have proved to be successful ways for parents to communicate with other parents about similar concerns. For example, Yahoo! Groups has hundreds of support groups for different conditions that affect children. There is also the possibility of starting your own group on the internet. A good, active group with a varied group of members can provide answers to questions and advice that may not be available in any book or official website. There can also be the satisfaction of being able to help others with your discoveries along your journey. www.groups.yahoo.com

Some support organisations have local groups or local representatives who can help in person. Often, local sources of support are known best to health visitors and volunteer bureaux (these go under different names; the public library can direct you to your nearest volunteer bureau). Increasingly, local councils are building internet sites containing information about all the services they know of in the area; search under the name of your local council. There are also many search engines on the internet – www.search.msn.com www.yahoo.com www.excite.com – to name a few. One only needs to enter the condition of your child in the search engine to find a host of resources that are available.

h) YOUTH SERVICES

There are a number of organisations for children and young people that encourage children with disabilities to participate and are good examples of inclusion. If there is a need for an assistant to help your child in order to participate in these groups, it is worth asking Social Services for help.

Girl Guides – Girlguiding UK is the largest organisation for girls and young women in the UK.
http://www.guidingessentials.org.uk/mall/departmentpage.cfm/GirlGuiding

Scouts – including Beavers, Cubs and Scouts, and have groups throughout the UK. In some areas there are Disabled Scout Groups. www.scoutbase.org.uk
Duke of Edinburgh Award Scheme – the award can be done by absolutely anyone aged fourteen to twenty-five. They have a Bronze award, Silver and Gold Awards. Young people with disabilities have achieved all three awards. The award is often run at schools and colleges, the local youth club, or in a uniformed youth organisation like the Scouts or Guides. www.theaward.org

The Prince's Trust – provide an opportunity for young persons between the ages of sixteen to twenty-five who are unemployed to join a team of fifteen people for twelve weeks. They spend an action packed week at a residential home, take on community projects and get two weeks of work experience. They learn practical skills, make new friends and get a national recognised qualification. The course is free and is at over three hundred locations around the UK. Being on the course does not affect any benefits the young person receives. www.princes-trust.org.uk

Disability Sports – Disability Sport England is an organisation that provides opportunities to participate in sport for people with a disability. They provide an annual calendar of twelve national championships and over two hundred regional events as well as junior and senior programmes. In Wales, Disability Sport Cymru, in Scotland, Scottish Disability Sport www.scottishdisabilitysport.com and in Northern Ireland, Disability Sport NI have a similar function. Many local authorities now have a Disability Sport Development officer.

i) EMPLOYMENT RELATED SERVICES

Help with looking for employment may include advice and help in finding a job, extra training, and knowledge of any supported employment scheme in your area, special equipment that may be needed, and transport to the place of employment. Social Services should know about any supported employment schemes.

The Jobcentre or Jobcentre Plus will have a Disability Employment Advisor (DEA). They can offer an employment assessment to find out how the disability would affect the type of work or training that the person wants to do. They will also know about special programmes to help disabled people find suitable work. They will have information on the Job Introduction Scheme that places people in jobs for a trial period and pays the employer a grant during that period to see if they are suitable for the job.

Other organisations that can give advice and help with employment are:

Skill (National Bureau for Students with Disabilities) provides information and advice relating to post sixteen vocational, further and higher education, and training and employment opportunities – www.skill.org.uk

Shaw Trust has employment projects to help disabled people realise their potential – www.shaw-trust.org.uk

Remploy provides employment opportunities for disabled people across the UK both within their factories and in many other host organisations. – www.remploy.co.uk

Rathbone provides vocational training and employment opportunities – www.rathbonetraining.co.uk

Links:
Jobcentre and Jobcentre Plus – www.jobcentreplus.gov.uk
Careers Scotland – www.careers-scotland.org.uk
Connexions – www.connexions.gov.uk
Careers Wales – www.careerswales.com
Department of Employment and Learning Northern Ireland – www.delni.gov.uk

Resource:
After 16 – What's New – www.after16.org.uk An excellent source of information for young disabled people and their parents and carers to help them make decisions about the future. It is also available for free in book form.

j) SUMMARY

This section has outlined the statutory and major voluntary welfare services available to families and children with disabling conditions. If you are aware of a gap in provision, either because there is no service or the one provided does not meet yours and others needs very well, then voluntary organisations in the relevant fields may be able to take up the idea, or you may like to approach services directly to see what else can be done.

Search engines on the Internet, to name a few. You only need to enter the condition of your child in the search engine to find a host of resources that are available:

www.google.com   www.search.msn.com   www.yahoo.com

SECTION C – PROCESSES IN EDUCATION

a) STRUCTURE OF THE EDUCATION SYSTEM AND SOURCES OF SUPPORT

Local Education Authority facilities come under the Education Act and general children's legislation, as well as local government legislation and codes of practice. In each UK region there is a code of practice for special educational needs which is more detailed secondary legislation guiding the identification of, and provision for, children/students under nineteen years who may need extra help with learning.

Local Education Authorities oversee provision and standards of education in:

- Crèches,
- Nursery schools,
- Special and Mainstream schools,
- Further Education colleges,
- Community education classes,
- Local hospital education facilities,
- Homes in which children are educated,
- Children's residential facilities.

They have a legal responsibility to ensure that all children receive the relevant education, although the primary responsibility remains with parents/guardians. The Local Education Authority's role is limited in non-school environments and privately-funded schools. It is, in effect, the education department of the Local

Authority and employs most staff involved in education; it is headed by a director who is responsible to the elected local councillors and the national government department for education.

Local authorities are also responsible for the allocation of:
• Student grants and scholarships,
• School transport,
• Support for education personnel and school governors,
• Upkeep and cleaning of premises,
• Clothing grants,
• Free school milk and meals,
• Catering,
• The music service for instrumental lessons,
• Provision for sensory impairment,
• Information technology,
• Education for children using minority languages.

And, in Wales:

• Education provision through the medium of Welsh and English.
  Parents can contact them directly for information about any of these, or help about a school or college.
  Other educational facilities can be found in the Yellow Pages under '**Educational Services**' in the telephone book and the local section of the public library. Some private enterprises, such as dyslexia services or tutoring, may charge highly for their services, whilst those run by voluntary organisations or attached to national schemes and local councils may charge little or nothing.
  '**Special Needs Advisors**' work directly for pupils in special schools, and can also help careers advisors in mainstream schools and colleges, and parents making decisions on the next step for their children. Contact details can be found under names such as 'Education & Employment', 'Department for', 'Learning Direct', 'Careers Wales' and Connexions in the telephone directory or, alternatively, through a free-phone line 0800 100 900.

Educational psychologists work for the local authority and others operate privately. If a nursery or school require a consultation for a child having learning or development difficulties, this should only be done if the child is under sixteen with the parents' consent, or with the child's consent for those over sixteen. Consenting parties should receive copies of any reports. Parents have a right to be present when the psychologist sees their child.

Parents are entitled to contact educational psychology service directly, although they will still work through the nursery or school. Private psychologists will charge to see children, but LEAs are not obligated to accept their reports if they differ from their own findings.

Schools also have access to advisors for matters such as:
* Development,
* Behaviour management,
* Languages and computers.

And from the health sector:
* The children's mental health team,
* Nurses,
* Occupational, Speech and Physical Therapists.

Information and Advice Sources

LEAs must make arrangements for providing parents of children with special educational needs with information, and publicise the service to parents, schools and others. Each LEA in England and Wales has a parent partnership scheme (which may have a different title), conforming to the revised Code of Practice for Special Educational Needs. They can help families to understand and use the system, if necessary, accompanying you to meetings and putting you in touch with other services, while attempting to prevent or minimise disputes. You do not have to have a problem to consult them as they can also help over the details of the local situation and what is there, or can be put in place, that could be of further benefit to a child. They are independent of the administration of the LEA but in most cases receive annual funding from the local authority. This has led to concern about their freedom to support parents and children in cases of serious disagreement with the school or LEA. Therefore, sometimes parents prefer to consult a national educational advice body. The DFES (Department for Education and Skills, previously the DfEE) and the DRC (Disability Rights Commission) provide a range of advice, as do a number of voluntary organisations.

b) CHOICE OF TYPE OF EDUCATION

Whilst the UK retains its mixture of mainstream, special and other education, the trend now is to encourage as many children as possible to be educated in mainstream rather than special education. However, parents can still choose a non-mainstream form of education if they want and the LEA can also choose to offer other provision if a child has severe problems that affect the education of other children, particularly behavioural ones. It may be either funded by the LEA or by another party (such as parents themselves), and it is also possible for a child without a Statement to attend a special school while they are being assessed, or if the headteacher, LEA and parents all agree to it because of circumstances. The LEA has to be satisfied (1) that the choice will enable the child to receive the provision that is needed for them; (2) that nothing will stop other children from receiving appropriate provision as well; and (3) that the placement is an efficient use of the Authority's resources.

c) EDUCATION AT HOME

There is a great deal of advice and material available for use in home education, including libraries, the Internet and trips out.

A good setting-off point is: http://www.home-education.org.uk with links to the Home Education Advisory Service and the BBC Education section. From there, the National Grid for Learning has many resources on the Internet and the membership organisation 'Education Otherwise' provides materials, support and a network of groups where parents and children who are home-educating can meet.

Other Useful Websites and Addresses
Relate is an organisation that offers mediation and counselling for relationship problems, more than just 'marriage guidance'. The national helpline is 0845 130 4010 or for local offices see Yellow Pages.

Family Mediation Centres – see local Yellow Pages and public libraries (the local centre might have a different name).

d) USEFUL WEB LINKS AND TELEPHONE NUMBERS

www.dataprotection.gov.uk

www.hmso.gov.uk

www.doh.gov.uk/directpayments

www.tiger.gov.uk provides easy access to information on all points of employment laws in relation to parental rights. Information for working parents can be found on:

www.parentsatwork.org.uk

www.justask.co.uk

www.lcd.gov.uk

Family Rights Group www.frg.org.uk

Dads UK, for single fathers www.dads-uk.co.uk

One Parent Families Organisation www.oneparentfamilies.org.uk

www.childsupportanalysis.co.uk

www.nfpi.org/data/publications/index.htm#healthmaze

Working Parents – 0207 253 4664

ACAS mediation service, national advice line 0845 47 47 47

www.acas.org.uk

Equal Opportunities Commission – 0845 601 5901

www.eoc.org.uk

www.dti.gov.uk

www.carersonline.org.uk

Gingerbread runs self-help groups for lone parents with over two hundred local groups. Advice line – 0800 018 4318 www.gingerbread.org.uk

www.raisingkids.org.uk offers advice, information and parent chat forums.

Parent Line Plus provides general support for parents, grandparents, guardians and foster parents. Telephone 0808 800 2222 or www.parentline.org.uk

The Children's Legal Centre offers free advice on laws affecting children and those that care for them

www.childrenslegalcentre.com

The Disabled Parents' Network deals with problems faced by disabled parents and their families.

www.disabledparentnetwork.org.uk

National Association for Child Support Action is a lobby group campaigning for a fairer child support system. www.nacsa.org.uk

The BBC has informative websites on health, education, legal and other personal issues, along with specific action lines dealing with enquiries. www.bbc.co.uk

N.B.

Now that you have pinpointed your information source and approached them, do not forget to evaluate the information that they have given to you. Something may invalidate your newly acquired knowledge, such as it being out of date. Always check the dates of books, magazines, newspapers, and when Internet sources were last updated. Outdated information may be misleading. Different types of information take different lengths of time to need updating, but most of what you will need is likely to be more useful if it is not more than a year old. Information providers should screen what they are sending you, and libraries try to keep directories etc. up to date, but there will still be books, web sites and information you have collected yourself some time ago, that do not contain the most recent information. For instance, the financial and welfare benefits world tends to adjust its payments and systems at the beginning of its year, during April and May.

Particularly when using the Internet, be very careful. Make sure that the information that you are obtaining applies to this country. Many Internet sites are American and, especially in the case of legal information, may not be correct when applied to the UK. It is also advisable to be watchful with information within the UK. Scotland has different circumstances and laws from the rest of the UK. In the case of government funded services, it is also advisable to be aware that there are probably regional differences.

Simply because something is in the public domain does not mean that it is accurate or true. Professionals who know about particular subjects, quality standards of various kinds and signs of reliability that you can recognise, are a help to assessing how much to rely on information that is put before you. Information professionals in voluntary organisations and libraries can also help. Increasingly the major services are recognising the need of people who seek out their information, and are taking steps to provide guidance.

CHAPTER 9

FINAL THOUGHTS

There are, as we have seen, two types of stress namely, eustress (the good stress) and distress (the bad stress). The former is the more common of the two as it is essential to our everyday lives. It is eustress which motivates and stimulates, prevents lethargy and enables the individual to get out of bed every morning and face the challenges of a new day. The second type, distress, is the one we are more aware of as it occurs when we feel that we cannot cope. We are also made aware of our distress levels rising by the signs and symptoms it triggers.

There are few people who do not experience periods of high stress during their lives and parents with a brain-injured child are particularly vulnerable. They are not only charged with the general care and welfare of their son/daughter but often have to act as nurse, doctor and many other roles as well. To compound the situation, many have to fulfil their roles as parent/carer without the necessary support. Fortunately, the compensating qualities of love and joy that the child brings, help to mitigate the stress. Nevertheless, action needs to be taken to address the problems.

A large percentage of the perceived factors which cause the stress are 'external' and could be overcome by providing unlimited resources which would enable the parents to receive maximum support at all times. This is currently not possible and seems to be very unlikely to happen in the foreseeable future. It would, however, be a major step forward if the resources that are available were used more efficiently and effectively.

- There appears to be a great need for a 'joined up approach' where all of the support services could work together to provide the best possible support for each individual case and where bureaucracy is not allowed to prevent or delay a family from receiving appropriate help at the time it is required.

- There needs to be more accessible, easy to understand, and comprehensive information about both the diagnosis and the benefit support that are available, as well as details of how to make an application for this support. Additionally, the information needs to be cross-linked. For example, it should advise parents that if they have successfully applied for benefits A and B, then they are also entitled to apply for benefits X and Y.

- Every parent with a brain-injured child should be allocated a named key worker who would be responsible for coordinating the various services and offering general advice.

- It appears that the training courses for the professionals who come into contact with the parents and children do not currently cover all of the skills necessary to address the current areas of dissatisfaction identified by the parents in Chapter 2. Better communication skills and mutual respect are essential to the effectiveness of the relationships with professionals.

- Whilst discrimination is currently not a major issue identified by the parents we must not become complacent. The enactment of the Disability Discrimination Act must continue to ensure that the basic rights of the children are met. This includes the provision of accessible holiday accommodation and out of school leisure activities, both of which appear to be currently lacking.

- In the meantime, parents must address the internal causes of their high stress levels. They can do this by being proactive and taking care of their general health and well-being, learning to change their perceptions of what are now seen as stressful situations and mastering relaxation techniques so that they can be called upon, as and when, needed.

The author has been working in the area of 'stress' for over twenty years but has never before witnessed such genuine warmth and optimism from a group of people who have gained her respect and admiration. In her opinion, these parents have every right to feel let down by the very system that is there to support them. She is grateful to them for letting her share their experiences of caring for their special children and hopes that this book will make at least a small contribution to making their lives a little easier.

FURTHER READING

This book was not written as a textbook but as a guide for parents trying to cope with stress. There are a large number of texts which may be of interest to those wishing to delve a little deeper. The following books have proved to be popular with individuals seeking to make some changes to their lives in order to lower their stress levels.

- LINDENFIELD G (2001) *Assert Yourself*
  Harper Collins
  ISBN 0007123450

- LOOKER T and GREGSON 0 (2003) *Managing Stress*
  Teach Yourself Books
  Hodder and Stoughton
  ISBN 0340860073

- POWELL T (2004) *Head Injury. A practical Guide*
  Speechmark Publishing Ltd.
  ISBN 0-86388-451-2

- RICE P L (1992) *Stress and Health*
  Brooks/Cole Publishing Co.
  ISBN 0-535-17280-6

- ROLAND P (2002) *How to Meditate: Combat Stress and Harness the Power of Positive Thought*
  Hamlyn Pyramid Paperbacks
  ISBN 060061221

- SACHS J (1998) *Break the Stress Cycle. 10 Steps For Reducing Stress for Women*
  Adams Media Corporation
  ISBN 9-781580-620079

- SUTTON J (1998) *Thriving on Stress. How to Manage Pressures and Transform Your Life*
  How To Books Ltd.
  ISBN 1-85703-238-1

- WILKINSON G (1997) *Understanding Stress*
  Family Doctor Publications
  ISBN 1-898205-38-8

QUESTIONNAIRE

On the following pages there is a copy of the questionnaire used for the research – the results of which are reported in Chapter 2.

Dear Parent,

Thank you for taking the time to read this letter. I am very aware of the additional associated challenges that face parents raising a brain-injured child and I am trying to find ways of helping you to overcome some of these problems. In order to do this I must gain an insight into the types of issues which cause you most stress. I also need to identify the supportive information that you would like to see more readily available in a user friendly pack. To do this I am asking approximately four thousand parents with a child with a brain related condition if they would assist me by completing the attached questionnaire. **Cerebra**, a charity committed to helping brain injured children and their parents, are sponsoring this research and are distributing most of these questionnaires for me. This guarantees that <u>I will not learn of your identity unless you volunteer it.</u>

As soon as I have analysed the results from the questionnaires I am hoping to have informal meetings or telephone conversations with as many parents as possible to ensure that I have fully understood your main concerns. It would help me considerably, therefore, if you would complete the final question on page 8 in order that I can contact you personally in a few months time. After you have completed the questionnaire please return it to me in the stamped addressed envelope provided. The final results will be published by Cerebra. If you have any queries please do not hesitate to contact me on **01792 481252** or e-mail me at <u>ann.edworthy@sihe.ac.uk</u>

Your support and help is greatly appreciated.

Dr Ann Edworthy

Section A

1. In general, how stressful do you find your role as a parent of a brain-injured child ? (Please circle the appropriate number) PLEASE NOTE THERE ARE QUESTIONS ON BOTH SIDES OF THE PAGE

Not stressful	1	Appreciably Stressful	3
Mildly Stressful	2	Extremely Stressful	4

2. Are there any particular times of the week, or year, that are more stressful for

you than others? If yes please state the most stressful times.

Section B

For each of the following factors, please circle the number appropriate to the degree of stress you experience in relation to it.

	No Stress	Mild Stress	Appreciable Stress	Extreme Stress	Not Applicable
1. Practical problems eg. Transport, in taking your child to the doctors /dentist /hospital.	1	2	3	4	5
2. Communications between you and the GP	1	2	3	4	5
3. Communications between you and the child's consultant.	1	2	3	4	5
4. Communications between you and the School.	1	2	3	4	5
5. Communications between you and your brain-injured child.	1	2	3	4	5
6. Apparent lack of understanding from your employer.	1	2	3	4	5
7. The amount of financial support/benefits from the state.	1	2	3	4	5
8. The amount of general advice readily available eg a written guide on where to go for different types of help.	1	2	3	4	5
9. The amount of practical support available e.g. respite care.	1	2	3	4	5

	1	2	3	4	5
10. Coming to terms with the prognosis of your child i.e. what the future holds for your child.	1	2	3	4	5
11. Coming to terms with the diagnosis of your child.	1	2	3	4	5
12. Level of responsibility in caring for the child e.g. administering medicine/physiotherapy.	1	2	3	4	5
13. Devoting time and resources to other family members.	1	2	3	4	5
14. Sleepless nights(due to 24 hour care needed by your disabled child).	1	2	3	4	5
15. Behaviour of the general public towards you and your disabled child.	1	2	3	4	5
16. Your child's distress due to his/her illness.	1	2	3	4	5
17. The amount of equipment needed and the space it occupies.	1	2	3	4	5
18. Lifting and handling your disabled child.	1	2	3	4	5
19. Amount of leisure time at your disposal.	1	2	3	4	5
20. The practicalities of taking a holiday.	1	2	3	4	5
21. Concern about your child's future as you grow older.	1	2	3	4	5
22. Concern that your child does not have a happy childhood.	1	2	3	4	5
23. Worry that your child may be lonely.	1	2	3	4	5
24. Concern that your relationship with your partner/spouse is suffering as a result of the pressures of having a brain-injured child.	1	2	3	4	5
25. Worry that your own health will suffer.	1	2	3	4	5
26. Illness of another family member.	1	2	3	4	5
27. Practicalities of everyday tasks. eg Shopping	1	2	3	4	5

22. Receiving mail about baby products etc as a new parent.	1	2	3	4	5
23. Mobility level of your child.	1	2	3	4	5
24. Your child's coordination.	1	2	3	4	5
31. Coping with your child's difficult or violent behaviour.	1	2	3	4	5
25. Visiting family and friends	1	2	3	4	5
26. Worries about the cause of your child's condition.	1	2	3	4	5
27. Level of coordination between support services.	1	2	3	4	5
28. Criticism from family and friends.	1	2	3	4	5
29. Criticism from professionals.	1	2	3	4	5
30. Fear for child's safety. Eg talking to strangers	1	2	3	4	5
37. Other (Please list any other sources of stress and indicate the level of stress that each causes you	1	2	3	4	5

………………………………………..

………………………………………..

………………………………………..

………………………………………..

………………………………………..

………………………………………..

………………………………………..

Questionnaire

Section C

1. How many hours per week, on average, are you able to spend time relaxing/socialising/doing things that help you to unwind?

2. What sort of activities do you find most helping in 'unwinding'?

3. Are you a member of a 'support' group?

4. What type of information would you like to see more readily available (e.g. how to apply for respite care, how to obtain equipment/financial support)?

5. Please suggest any ways in which your role as a carer may be made less stressful.

Section D

BACKGROUND INFORMATION (This section is designed to help me identify if there are problems that affect some parents more than others in order for me to offer the most appropriate help to each group.)

1.   Are you   (Please circle the appropriate number)

| | Male | 1 | Female | 2 |

2.   Is your disabled child? (Please circle the appropriate number)

| | Male | 1 | Female | 2 |

3.   What age group does your disabled child belong to ? (Please circle the appropriate number)

0 - 3 Yrs	1	12 - 15 Yrs	4
4 - 7 Yrs	2	16 - 20 Yrs	5
8 - 11 Yrs	3	21 and over	6

4.   How many children under 16 years of age do you have living at home   _____

5.   Do you have any other dependants living at home (e.g. elderly relatives)?

YES / NO

6.   How many adults living at home are in employment ?   _____

7.   Do you receive help from an extended family (eg grandparents) or similar support?

YES / NO

Questionnaire

On a scale of 1 - 5 (with 1 being not important / helpful and 5 being extremely important / helpful) please indicate how important / helpful you would find each of the following:

a) Talking to another parent who is in a similar situation   1   2   3   4   5

b) Receiving help with practical problems e.g. how to obtain forms; who to contact for specific advice etc.   1   2   3   4   5

c) Receiving explanations of medical terms and issues from a sympathetic person   1   2   3   4   5

d) Service of a postal lending library for your needs   1   2   3   4   5

e) Service of a postal lending library for your child's needs   1   2   3   4   5

f) Being able to join a parent support Group   1   2   3   4   5

g) An opportunity to talk to relevant professionals and be able to ask questions.   1   2   3   4   5

h) To be able to talk, in confidence, to a counsellor to 'get things off your chest'   1   2   3   4   5

i) To learn techniques which you could use at home to help you to relax.   1   2   3   4   5

I would like to assure you that the information you have supplied in completing this questionnaire will be treated in the strictest of confidence. I would also like to take this opportunity to thank you for completing and returning the questionnaire in the enclosed prepaid envelope. If you are willing to talk to me in further detail about some of the issues raised, please supply you name and address or telephone number and I will contact you as soon as I am ready to begin the second stage of this project.
With Best Wishes
Ann Edworthy

Your Name
....(OPTIONAL)

Address
....(OPTIONAL).

Tel.No
....(OPTIONAL)

The final results will be made available to anyone who wishes to receive a copy.

Best wishes,

Ann Edworthy